JENNIFER GUEST

THE ART ACTIVITY BOOK FOR PSYCHOTHERAPEUTIC WORK

100 Illustrated CBT and Psychodynamic Handouts for Creative Therapeutic Work

Jessica Kingsley *Publishers*
London and Philadelphia

First published in 2017
by Jessica Kingsley Publishers
73 Collier Street
London N1 9BE, UK
and
400 Market Street, Suite 400
Philadelphia, PA 19106, USA

www.jkp.com

Copyright © Jennifer Guest 2017

Front cover image source: Jennifer Guest

All rights reserved. No part of this publication may be reproduced in any material form (including photocopying of
any pages other than the illustrated handouts, storing in any medium by electronic means or transmitting) without
the written permission of the copyright owner except in accordance with the provisions of the law or under terms
of a licence issued in the UK by the Copyright Licensing Agency Ltd. www.cla.co.uk or in overseas territories
by the relevant reproduction rights organisation, for details see www.ifrro.org. Applications for the copyright
owner's written permission to reproduce any part of this publication should be addressed to the publisher.

Warning: The doing of an unauthorised act in relation to a copyright work may
result in both a civil claim for damages and criminal prosecution.

All illustrated handouts may be photocopied and can be downloaded at www.jkp.com/
voucher using the code GUESTPSYCH for personal use with this programme, but may not
be reproduced for any other purposes without the permission of the publisher.

Library of Congress Cataloging in Publication Data
A CIP catalog record for this book is available from the Library of Congress

British Library Cataloguing in Publication Data
A CIP catalogue record for this book is available from the British Library

ISBN 978 1 78592 301 2
eISBN 978 1 78450 607 0

Printed and bound in Great Britain

Again for Jessamy and Oscar
(both still amazing and inspirational)

Acknowledgements

Thank you to all my clients and colleagues who I've had the pleasure of working with in this therapeutic world, and who have helped bring these worksheets to life. I'd like to express thanks to everyone who has devoted their career and more to helping others live happier and healthier lives. I've given credit to all theorists whose work has formed the basis for these worksheets. Thanks also to Sarah Hamlin and Alexandra Holmes, and everyone at Jessica Kingsley Publishers, for their part in enabling this book to become available to so many.

Contents

Introduction

These worksheets have come into being following many years of therapeutic work with clients within clinical practice. The aim of these was to combine aspects of psychotherapeutic ideas with aspects of creative arts, keeping aesthetics in mind. The book provides an opportunity for people to be inspired by the worksheets and to help with visual communication, either verbally or non-verbally. It's assumed that most practitioners will be familiar with the theoretical ideas mentioned in the chapters. They are included in order to provide the basic frameworks from which the worksheets have been developed.

Some worksheets ask specifically focused questions; others aim to act as springboards for creative exploration, in which therapeutic change can arise. There are no instructions about how to use these pages, other than for clients to respond to the questions and tasks posed on the worksheets; they are open for interpretation in whatever way is most helpful. Their aim is to be an aesthetically designed invitation for people to draw, paint or write their responses. Sometimes the worksheets may simply provide a visual focus for the issues being discussed. They can be valuable for work in the session, or for clients to complete at home. It can be greatly beneficial to encourage clients in becoming creative about their problems.

People can find it helpful, soothing and mindful to doodle or colour in whilst thinking about difficult or painful experiences, and this can be incredibly cathartic. Each page gives an opportunity for people to do this whilst simultaneously focusing on the discussion points. It's hoped that there will be an array of art materials available for clients to use with this book.

The worksheets have been divided up into the themes of the five chapters. There is much overlap, as many could be included in more than one chapter. The book isn't intended to be used from beginning to end, rather that specific pages are chosen by client or practitioner based on what would be the most helpful and relevant. It's assumed that people using this book would be working within the safe arenas of therapy; if anyone chooses to use this book in isolation, please ensure that access to appropriate professional support is available, in case of any unexpected emotional responses to the themes presented here.

Theoretical perspectives
Psychodynamic concepts

Psychodynamic ideas have evolved from the original psychoanalytical work of Freud, Jung and Klein. Freud focused on how the mind/personality is made up and operates. He believed we are made of three components: the id, responsible for satisfying our instincts; the super-ego, which is our moral compass; and our ego, which reconciles the conscious and the unconscious, along with our relationship with reality and our sense of identity. He believed we are shaped by our conscious and unconscious processes, and driven by internal instincts.

Later came the developments of object relations and attachment theories, through the work of Klein, Winnicott and Bowlby. There was a shift in focus towards the impact of previous relational dynamics; how caregiver relationships during infancy and early childhood affect the development of our sense of self and our adult relationships. Hartmann, Anna Freud, Kohet and Kernberg's work developed the shift away from ideas about internal unconscious struggles towards the less pathological concepts of adaptation, relationship-seeking and social integration (Burton and Davey 2003). This is described by Charura and Paul in *The Therapeutic Relationship Handbook* (2014, p.4): 'Psychodynamic/psychoanalytical psychology explores the dynamics between the conscious and unconscious parts of self and relations with the external world.'

The worksheets based on psychodynamic concepts are mainly intended to aid exploration around these early relational dynamics, formative experiences and important memories, and how these impact on individuals in adulthood, rather than focusing on current relational dynamics such as those involving the processes of transference and projection, or the intrapsychic developments of defence mechanisms. Kerry Thomas (1996, p.292) describes some of the essential ideas behind psychodynamic theory, which have underpinned many of these worksheets:

> It is individuals' subjective experience, in its full symbolic complexity, together with their own life-stories and their overall construction of a self, that are the raw data of psychodynamic explorations. It is a fundamental assumption of the psychodynamic perspective that individuals have...their own intricately developed meaning systems.

Cognitive behavioural therapy concepts

Basic components of cognitive behavioural therapy (CBT) are about how our thinking affects our feelings, physiology and behaviour. It focuses on the idea that it's our interpretations of experiences and events that influence our feelings, rather than the *actual* experience causing our emotions. As early as the first century AD, philosopher Epictetus stated how people were 'disturbed not by things but by the views which they take of them' (Trower et al. 1988, p.1). Our interpretations are subjective, interwoven with our beliefs and may or may not be realistic or helpful.

Core beliefs influence our perspectives and interpretations of experiences. Facilitating clients in increasing their awareness of these is invaluable, leading them from potentially being overwhelmed by high emotion to more logical and realistic ways of information processing. A second category of beliefs is defined as 'intermediate beliefs', and these are the rules, attitudes and assumptions that inform our thinking, which often we are not completely aware of (Beck 1967).

The third category of beliefs is 'automatic thoughts', and these are the ones continually running through our minds. They can become problematic if they tend to be negative, especially if they are around our self, our competencies, our capabilities and ultimately our self-worth (Beck 1967). Focusing attention and exploration on these to elicit change can be hugely beneficial and therapeutic.

The emphasis for change is around breaking these negative patterns of thinking or unrealistic beliefs. Often we're not completely aware of our core beliefs, which have their origins in childhood. Motivation for change arises from personal beliefs about ourselves, in our capabilities and that the outcome of our actions will be of value (Bandura 1982).

Cognitive restructuring involves clients raising their awareness of the interactions of these three distinct types of thinking to identify the nature of what these are, in order to bring about changes in their emotional life and behaviour. The worksheets here are based on CBT concepts aiming to help people explore and change some of these unhelpful thinking patterns.

Creative arts in therapy

It's well known that the creative arts can be invaluable in enhancing the therapeutic journey. In relation to using creativity in therapeutic situations, this is described by Pam Fisher (2014, p.107): 'The creative arts/psychotherapies offer a framework and potential for practitioner and client to develop and work at the deepest level of relationship. They are recommended to practitioners to provide a holding frame and ongoing deepened awareness of self and others.'

In her book *The Art Therapy Sourcebook*, Cathy A. Malchiodi (2007, p.228) also describes how the creative arts can be beneficial: '…to enhance therapy, move the individual to action, express thoughts, practice behaviors, and to help the client examine options.'

Art making

Expressing ourselves in non-verbal ways by producing artwork can be liberating and cathartic. Possessing artistic ability is not relevant as it's the *making* of art rather than the aesthetics of what is produced that is beneficial. Malchiodi explains some of these benefits:

> History shows us that individuals under great stress have been known to make art as a way to express and transform inner conflicts…to explore human suffering, to find meaning for their emotional struggles, and to seek transcendence. By making art and using our imaginations, we may find relief from fears, anxiety, and depression and discover new meaning in our lives. (2007, p.16)

It's believed that being creative in a visual way stimulates the right-hand side of the brain's thinking processes, responsible for visual and perceptual thinking. The left-hand part is where verbal and logical thinking happens, and because this part of the brain isn't involved in visual art making, the functional censoring and filtering of information is redundant. This can allow new insights to come forth, unencumbered by the limitations of language (Edwards 2008).

Images were important in the work of Freud, who recognised that our feelings and thoughts are mainly experienced in a visual way, and how 'art is closer to the unconscious because our visual perceptions predate our capacity for verbal exploration' (Malchiodi 2007, p.9). She goes on to explain how Jung used to use images of his clients' memories and dreams:

> He observed that by allowing a mood or problem to become personified or by representing it as an image through art, we can begin to understand it more clearly and deeply and to experience the emotions that are contained within it. Jung's philosophy has influenced the field of psychotherapy, which has relied heavily on the images of memories…and their connection to feelings in helping people work through emotional conflicts and problems. (p.9)

The borders of the worksheets also provide an opportunity for colouring in, to help facilitate the therapeutic process and relaxation. Many people find it a soothing way to calm anxieties, and this can be especially helpful if some of the content of the worksheet is focusing on a difficult memory or experience.

Creative writing

Whilst the main focus in this book is about art making, some worksheets invite descriptions of meanings and memories. These descriptions may be symbolic images or written language. Either form of expression can be an initial platform to create larger pieces of artwork or expanded pieces of creative writing. Dr Gail Simon (2011) has done extensive research into the beneficial value of using creative writing for its therapeutic benefits, after noticing how some clients find it difficult to verbally express themselves. The idea of creative writing and the benefits of this in therapy are explored in detail in Dr Gillie Bolton's book *The Therapeutic Potential of Creative Writing: Writing Myself* (2000).

The worksheets here are invitations for people to create their own images or pieces of writing; with the idea of people using them in whatever way is the most helpful to aid expression.

Chapter 1

Understanding Self

It's fundamental for our emotional wellbeing to develop sound sense of who we are. Knowing what makes us feel happy, fulfilled and stimulated can increase our emotional wellbeing and improve mental health. Being aware of what sustains and supports us through difficult times and challenging experiences can be vital in how well we cope and manage. Developing our self-awareness and understanding can be a lifelong process of personal growth: elements of ourselves are fluid and ever changing as we move through life absorbing and processing experiences. Some elements of ourselves can be more consistent; for example, enjoying an activity from an early age through into adulthood as it remains a passion.

In psychodynamic terms, the subjectivity through which we develop a sense of ourselves and the world is described by Kerry Thomas in 'The defensive self: A psychodynamic perspective' (1996, pp.284–285):

> Psychodynamics is concerned with the *how*, *when* and *to what end* we construct our internal, symbolic representations of the external world…the emphasis is individualistic, on the idiosyncrasies of each person's psychic reality rather than the commonalities of 'reality'…the external world is represented in internal worlds to constitute psychic reality and selfhood.

From a CBT perspective, the assumptions are that we make rational decisions, and that our beliefs, values and intentions of behaviour are generally from conscious levels of awareness. Our thoughts and feelings make up our idea of identity, unique to ourselves. These inform and create our belief systems and views of who we are. Some worksheets in this section focus on concepts, ideas or simply words to stimulate exploration into what they mean to us specifically. It's often only by giving attention to such ideas that we can start to grasp and recognise what is important to us. These understandings have massive implications for the choices we make in life and our behaviour. The aim of increasing our understanding is to make more informed choices, by becoming more consciously aware of who we are and what we want to make of our lives. In their chapter in the *Handbook of Counselling Psychology* Strawbridge and Woolfe (2003, pp.10–11) write:

> 'Self-actualisation' is a central value in humanistic psychology. It is understood not only as the potential driving development but also as a highly valued developmental goal…a holistic and developmental view of an individual's life, life-style and location in their life course is a crucial focus to help clients into 'self-actualisation' or helping them reach their potential.

Using creativity can help with the development of a sense of self in learning who we are and how to express ourselves. As explained by Malchiodi in her book *The Art Therapy Sourcebook*:

> The creative process is conducive to individuation, the process of reaching one's full potential, and offers the opportunity for growth and change. Making art is believed to help one become more flexible, to self-actualise, and to tap creative problem solving and intuition… In making a drawing or painting, we begin the process of exploring our beliefs. We may find the reason for pain or depression or identify sources of joy and creative potential. Art inevitably tells our personal stories in all their dimensions: our feelings, thoughts, experiences, values and beliefs. In the process of making these visible through art, we are offered a way to know ourselves from a new perspective and an opportunity to transform that perspective. (2007, pp.17, 21)

These worksheets aim to facilitate this process. Some invite explorations into who we are, increasing our understanding and awareness, to help us comprehend how we come to terms with experiences, what certain life aspects *mean* to us, what's important, and also to help identify areas for change.

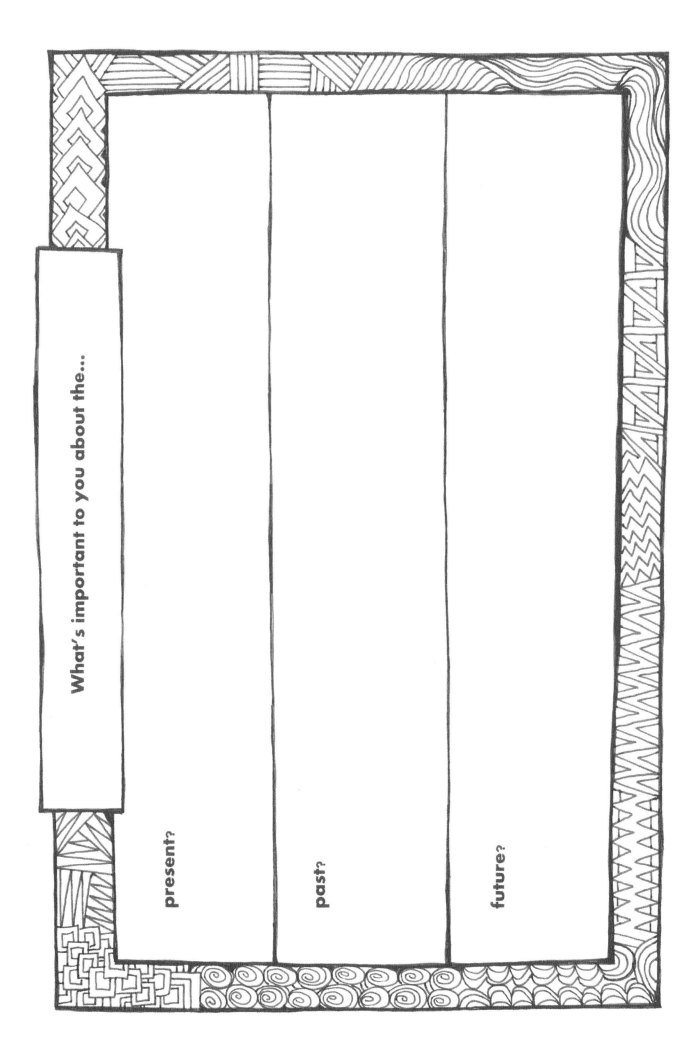

What's important to you about the...

present?

past?

future?

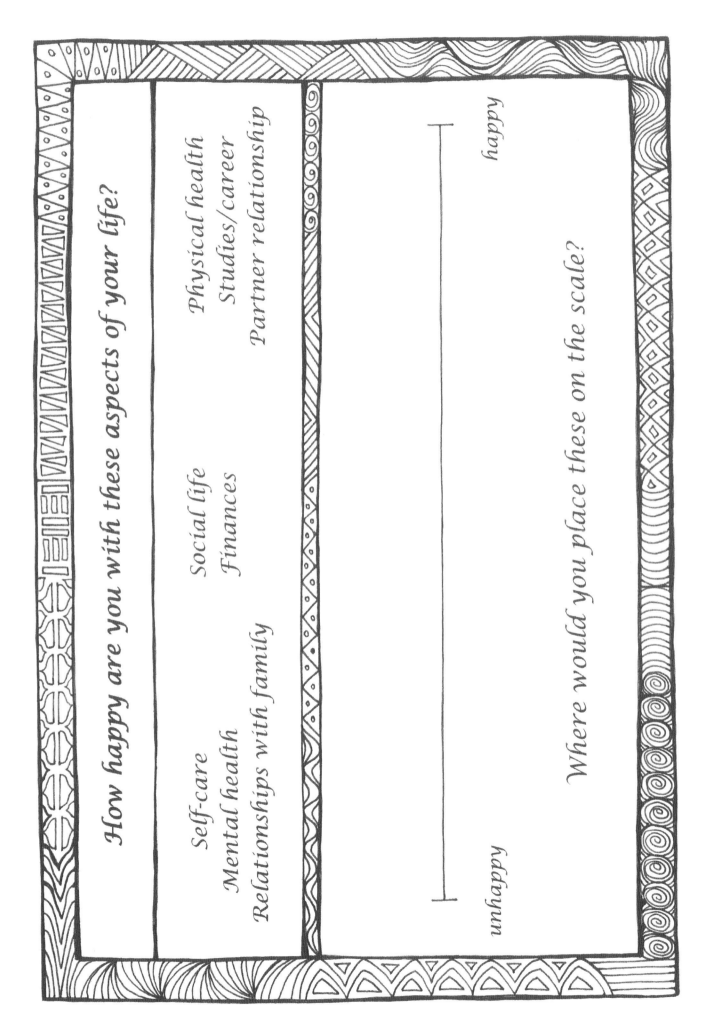

How happy are you with these aspects of your life?

Self-care
Mental health
Relationships with family

Social life
Finances

Physical health
Studies/career
Partner relationship

happy

unhappy

Where would you place these on the scale?

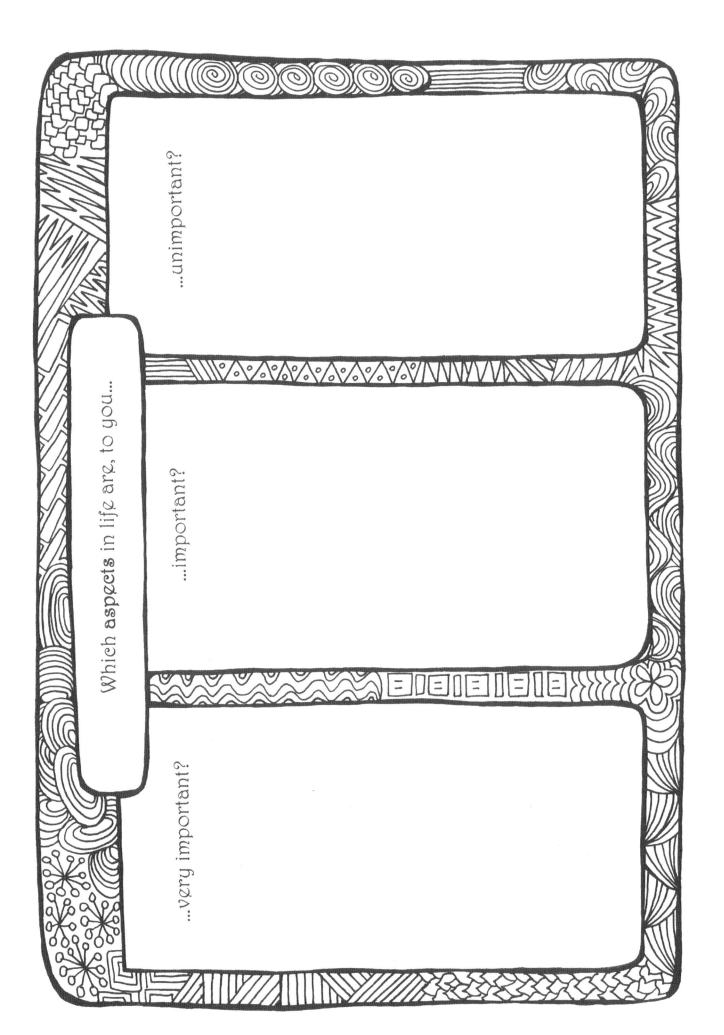

Which aspects in life are, to you...

...unimportant?

...important?

...very important?

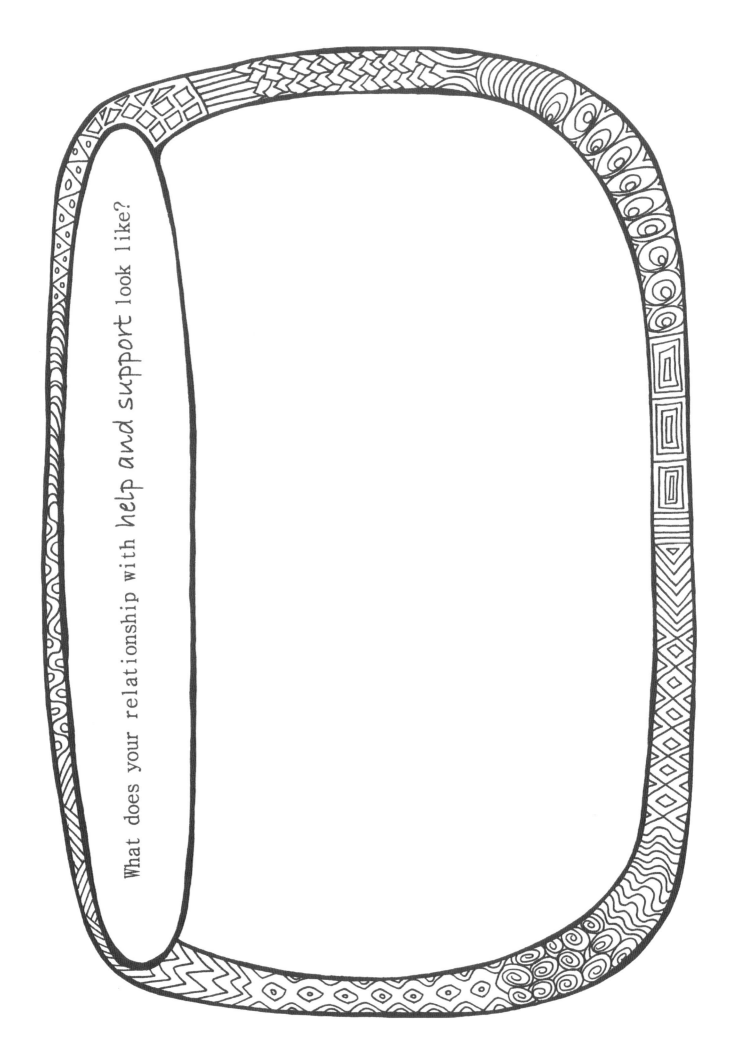

What does your relationship with *help and support* look like?

What are your experiences of endings?

What are your **emotional**
associations with endings?

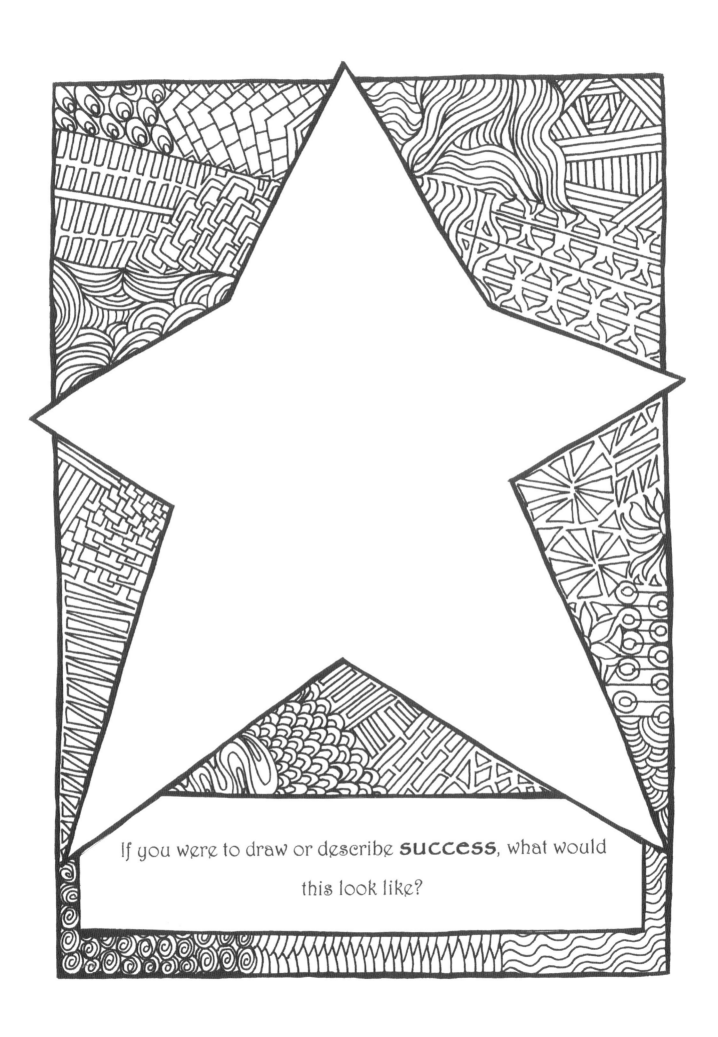

If you were to draw or describe **success**, what would this look like?

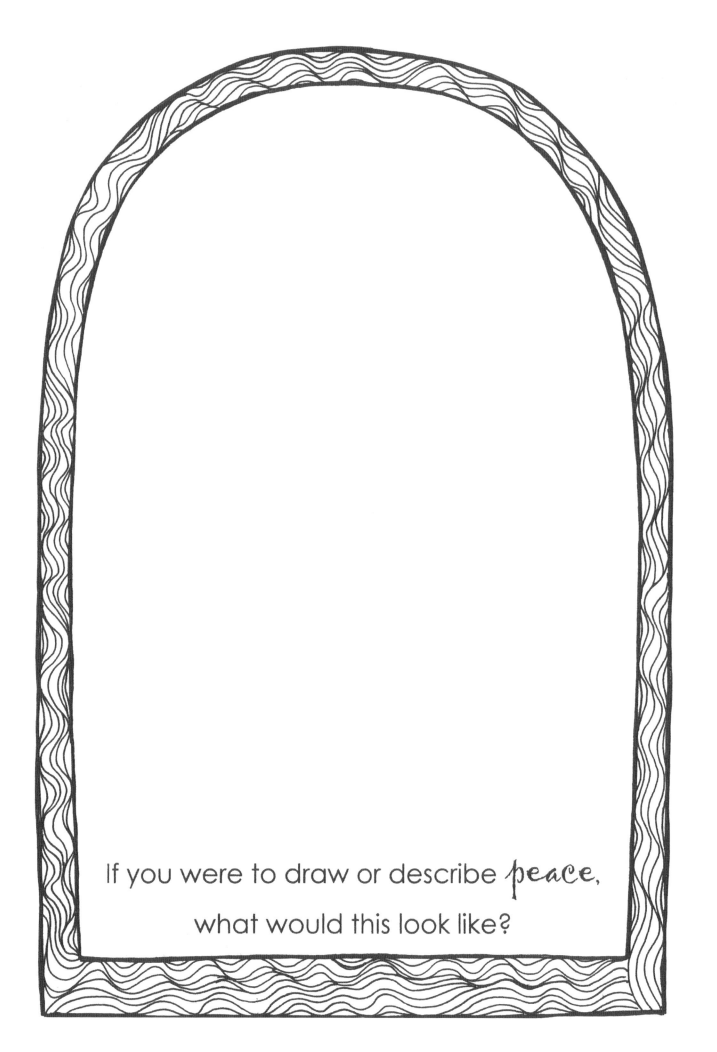

If you were to draw or describe *peace*, what would this look like?

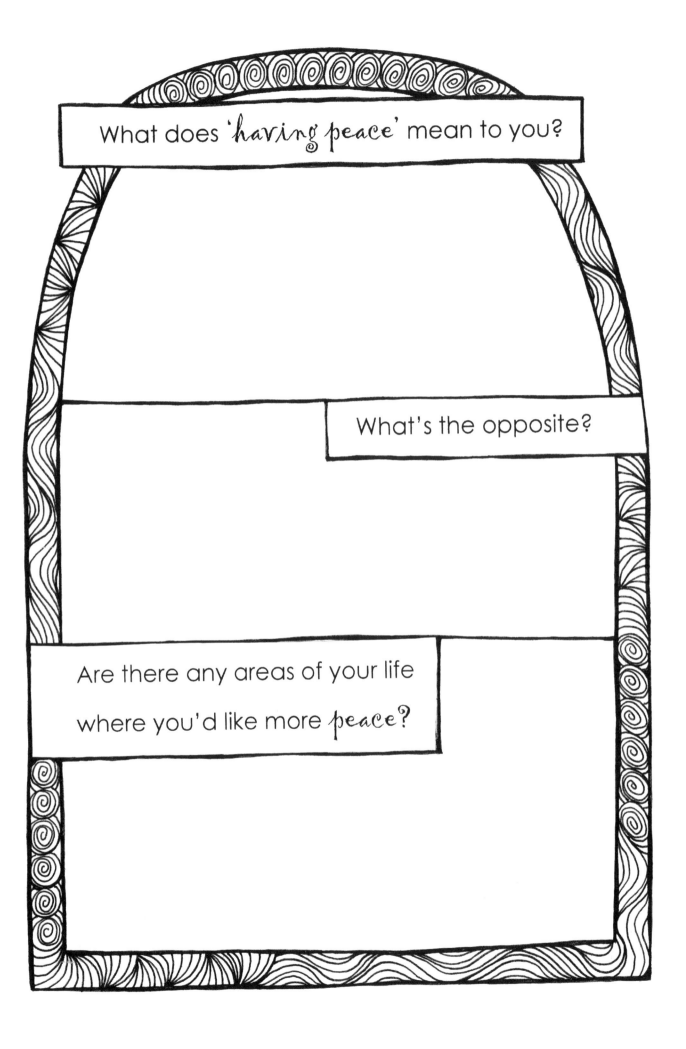

What does 'having peace' mean to you?

What's the opposite?

Are there any areas of your life where you'd like more peace?

My **home** *is a place where...*

Draw or describe how your **work-life** is

for you...

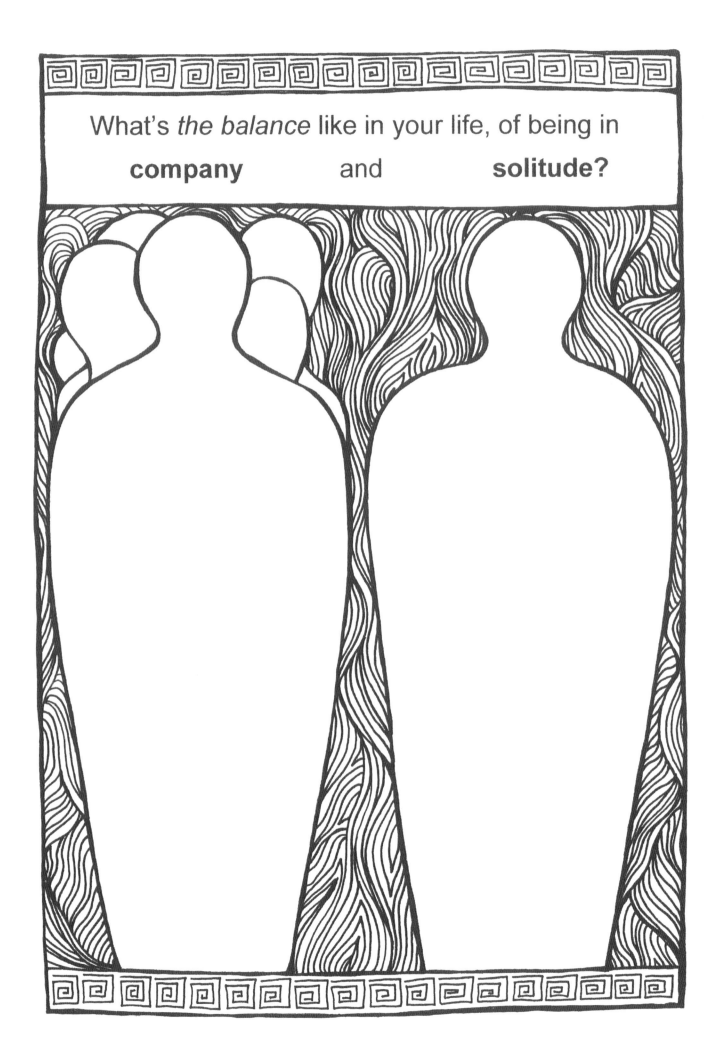

What's *the balance* like in your life, of being in **company** and **solitude?**

If you were to draw or describe **order**, what would this look like?

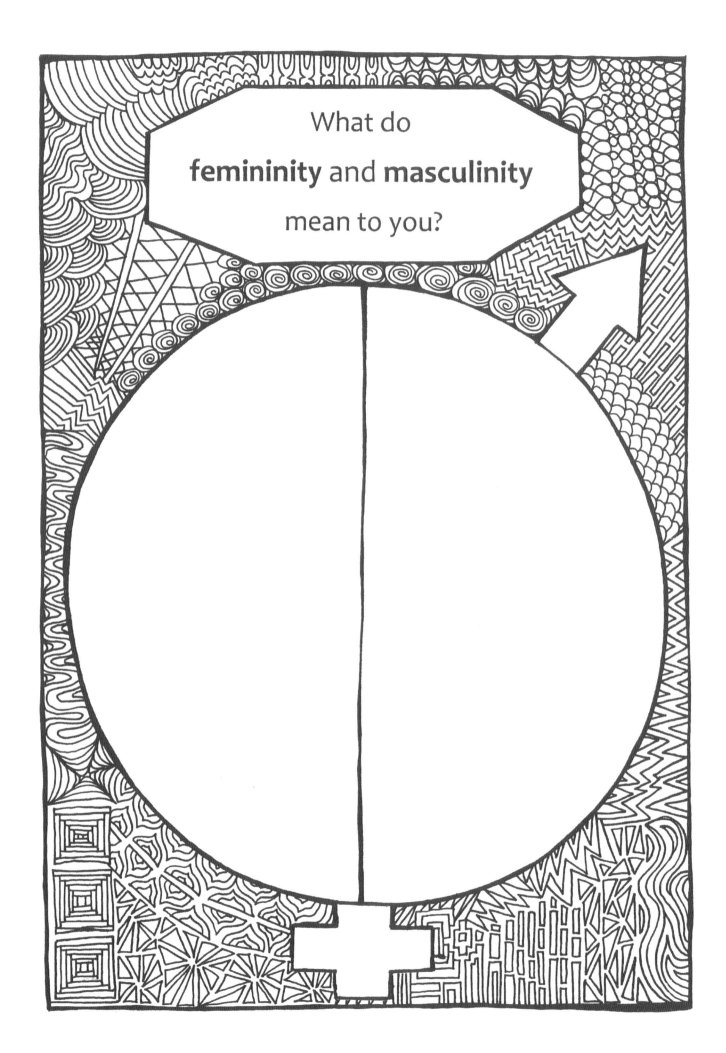

What do **femininity** and **masculinity** mean to you?

What's your idea of play and playfulness...

...in childhood?

...in adulthood?

What's the opposite of play and playfulness?

Where would you place yourself today on this continuum?

not playful ————————————————— playful

In which areas of your life are you more or less playful?

How important is **adventure** to you?

What's the opposite of **adventure**?

Do you have enough **adventure** in your life?

If you were to draw or describe **adventure**, what would this look like?

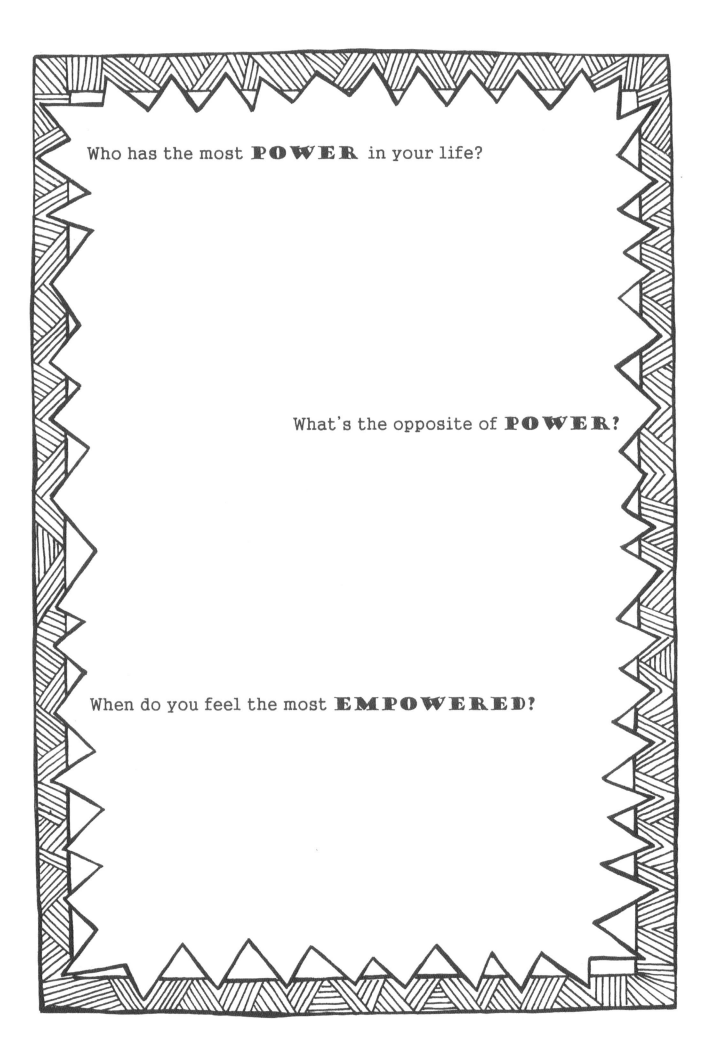

Who has the most **POWER** in your life?

What's the opposite of **POWER**?

When do you feel the most **EMPOWERED**?

If you were to draw or describe **POWER,** what would this look like?

Protection:

What would this look like in your life?

Protection:

How important is this to you?

What would the opposite look like?

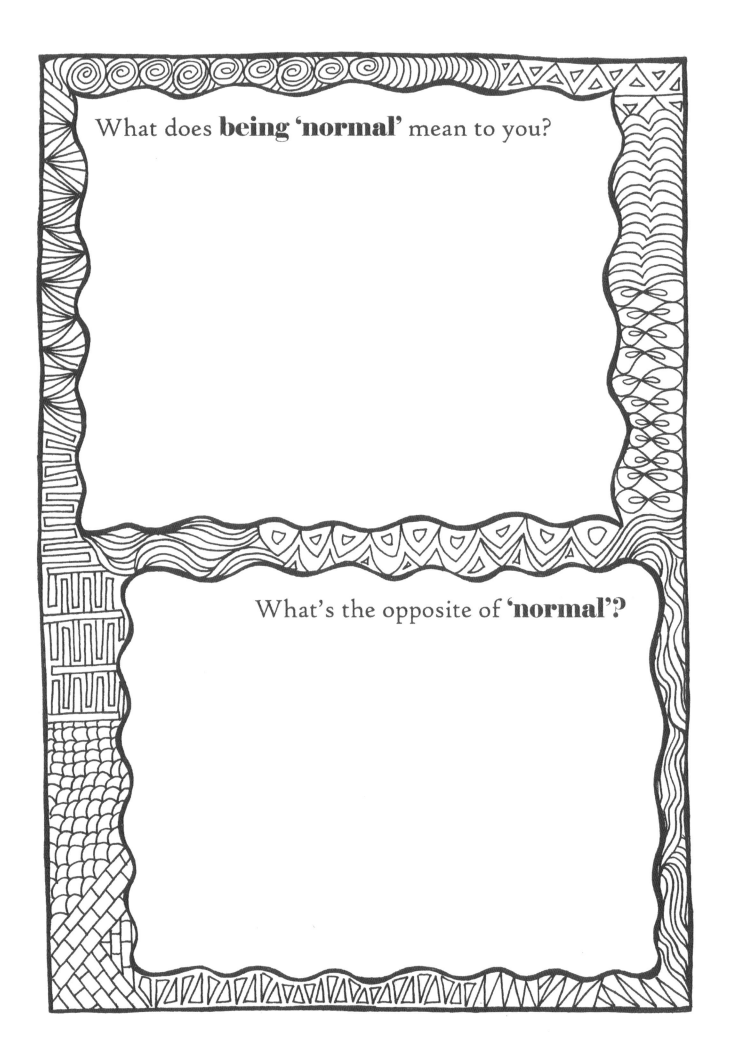

What does **being 'normal'** mean to you?

What's the opposite of **'normal'**?

How important is it for you to be *considered* as being **'normal'**...

...with friends?

...at work/school?

...with family?

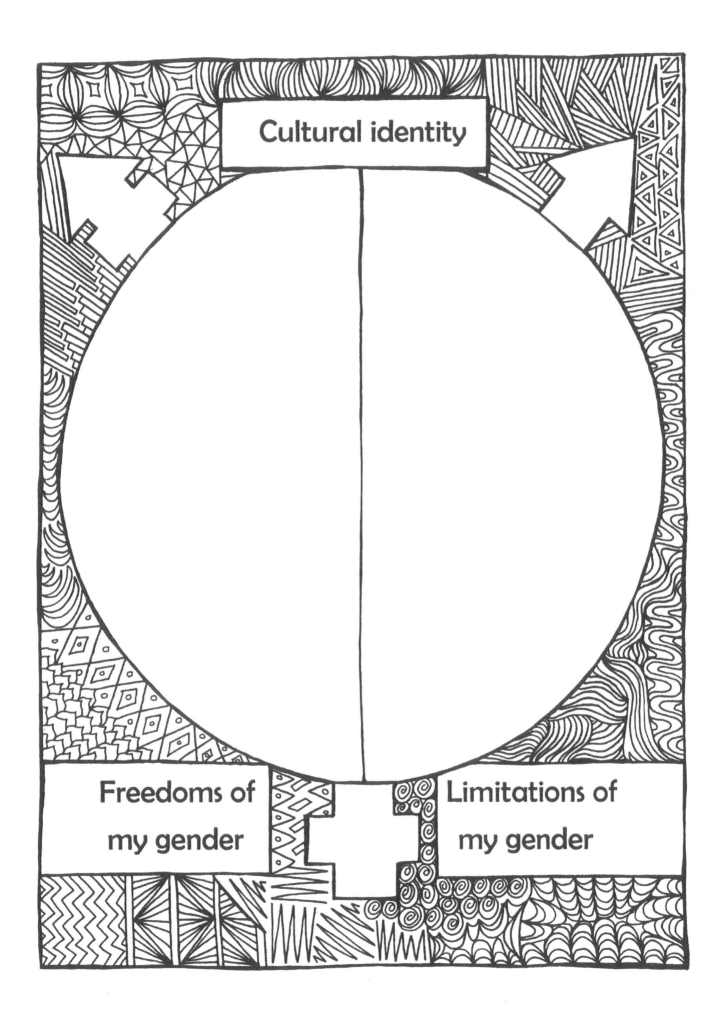

Cultural identity

Freedoms of
my gender

Limitations of
my gender

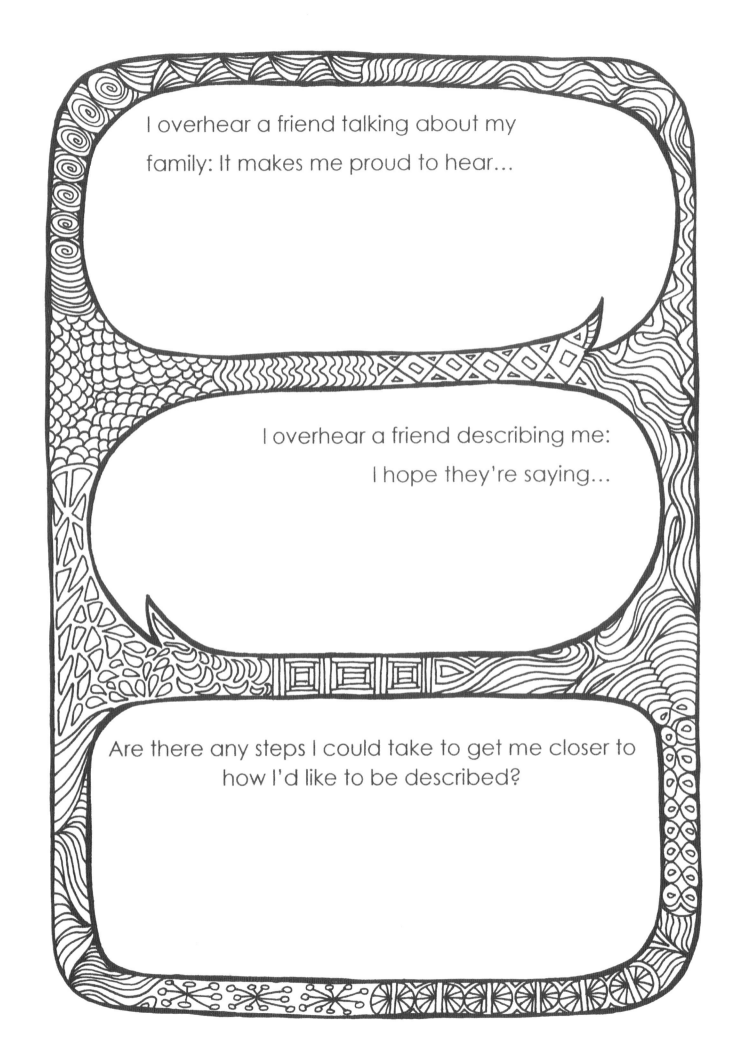

I overhear a friend talking about my family: It makes me proud to hear...

I overhear a friend describing me: I hope they're saying...

Are there any steps I could take to get me closer to how I'd like to be described?

Simplicity:

What would this look like in your life?

Chapter 2

Self-Esteem and Managing Emotions

The level to which we like and respect ourselves determines the amount of self-esteem we experience. If levels are low, we're likely to believe that we're less worthy or valued than others. Many external aspects can affect our self-esteem, such as stress, experiencing loss, receiving criticism or rejection, distressing experiences and other unexpected changes. Physical health problems can also have an impact on how we view ourselves. By becoming aware of our levels of self-esteem we can seek to raise our perceptions and care of ourselves. Using creative ways to provide this focus can be cathartic and healing. This is described by Pam Fisher (2014, p.100): '…creative arts processes have the potential to foster growth and change, and/or to support a client to be at their best…to *maximise wellness* in an individual.'

Beck et al. (1983) defined a difference between two types of personality in relation to cognitions and self-esteem: one type uses thoughts of achievement to help form their sense of self, whilst another type relies on the approval of those around them. These types can be described as autonomous and sociotropic (Scott and Dryden 2003). It's helpful for us to identify what's important to us in this respect: whether we rely on those around us to help boost our self-esteem, or if our own cognitions are affective.

Social scientist Roy Baumeister states in his book *Meanings in Life* (1991) that we have four basic needs that help us find meaning in life. These are purpose, value, efficacy and self-worth. Stevens and Wetherall write about this in their chapter in *Understanding the Self* (Stevens 1996): 'In Baumeister's view, self and identity becomes particularly significant as a source of meaning because our sense of self-worth and our sense of efficacy also depend on the way we think about our self' (Stevens and Wetherall 1996, p.343).

Our emotions make up a huge part of who we are. Learning to manage our feelings so that we aren't overwhelmed by them can be an essential part of increasing our wellbeing. In his book *Emotional Intelligence*, Daniel Goleman (1996, p.43) writes:

The ability to monitor feelings from moment to moment is crucial to psychological insight and self-understanding. An inability to notice our true feelings leaves us at their mercy. People with greater certainty about their feelings are better pilots of their lives, having a surer sense of how they really feel about personal decisions… People who are poor in this ability are constantly battling feelings of distress, while those who excel in it can bounce back far more quickly from life's setbacks and upsets.

By developing high levels of self-awareness, Goleman (1996, p.47) continues to explain how this prevents our perceptions from becoming distorted or over-dramatised; rather that 'it is a neutral mode that maintains a self-reflectiveness even amidst turbulent emotions…it manifests itself simply as a stepping-back from experience'.

Our emotional wellbeing and mental health are directly affected by our levels of self-esteem. Some worksheets in this chapter aim to help identify what these levels are and to increase self-worth. Others in this chapter aim to focus on how we connect with our emotional world and the processing of feelings. This is to encourage people to feel more in control and less at the mercy of strong emotion.

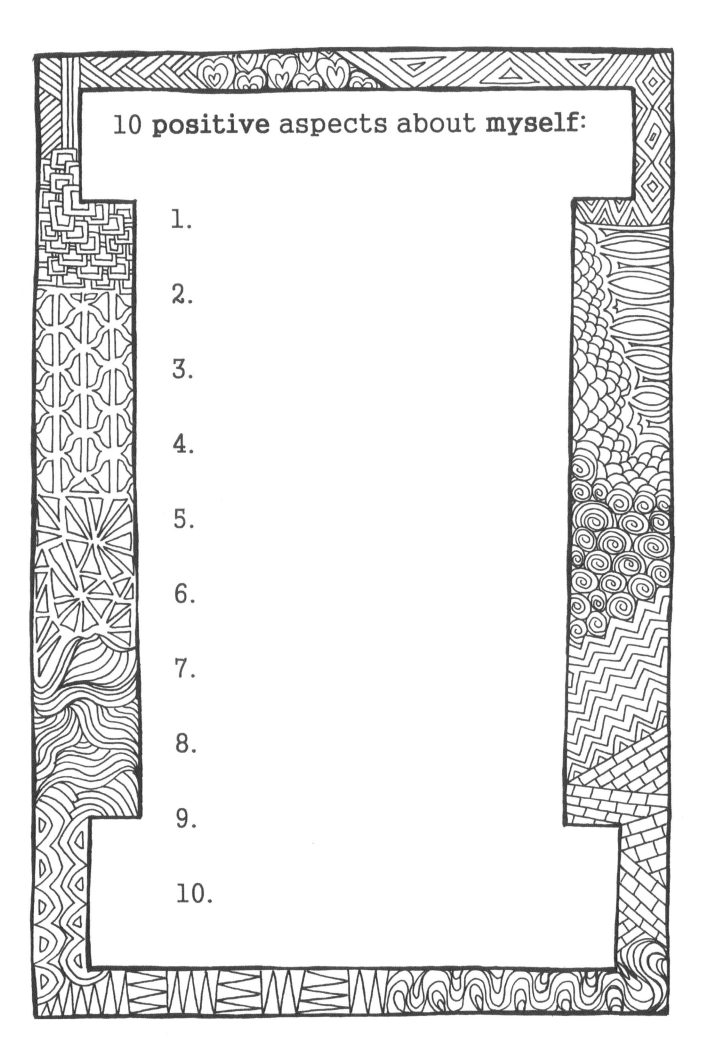

10 positive aspects about **myself:**

1.

2.

3.

4.

5.

6.

7.

8.

9.

10.

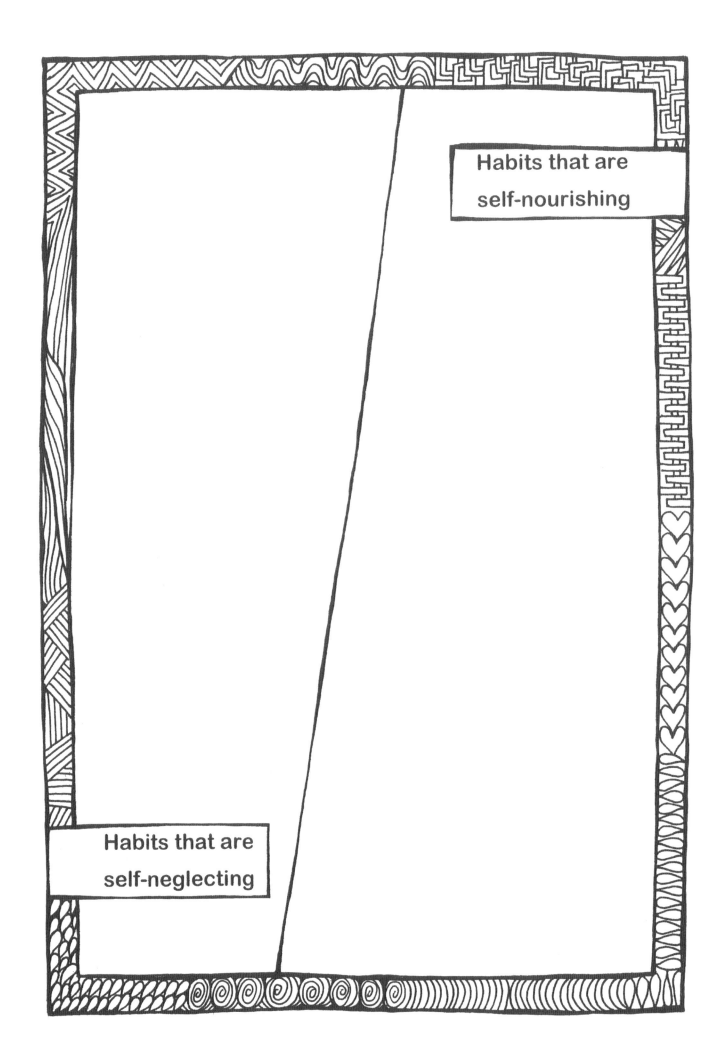

Habits that are
self-nourishing

Habits that are
self-neglecting

I feel proud of myself when...

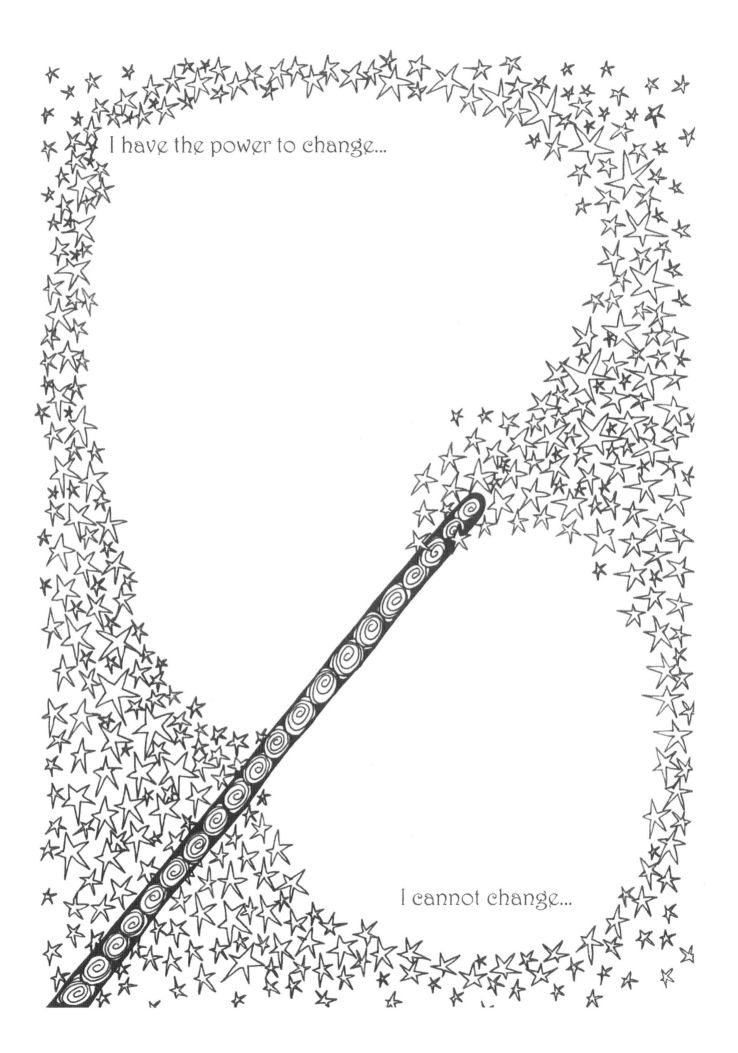

My achievements of the previous year

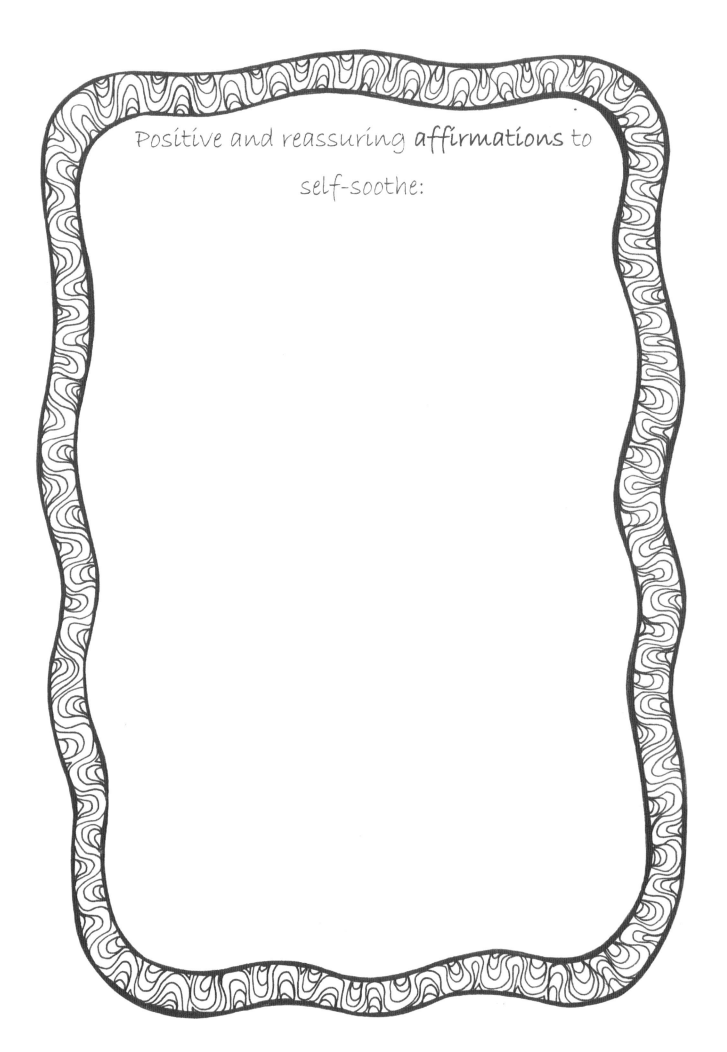

Positive and reassuring affirmations to self-soothe:

1.

2.

3.

4.

5.

6.

7.

8.

9.

10.

10 things I love about **my life...**

Draw or describe how *you'd like to be* in 5 years' time...

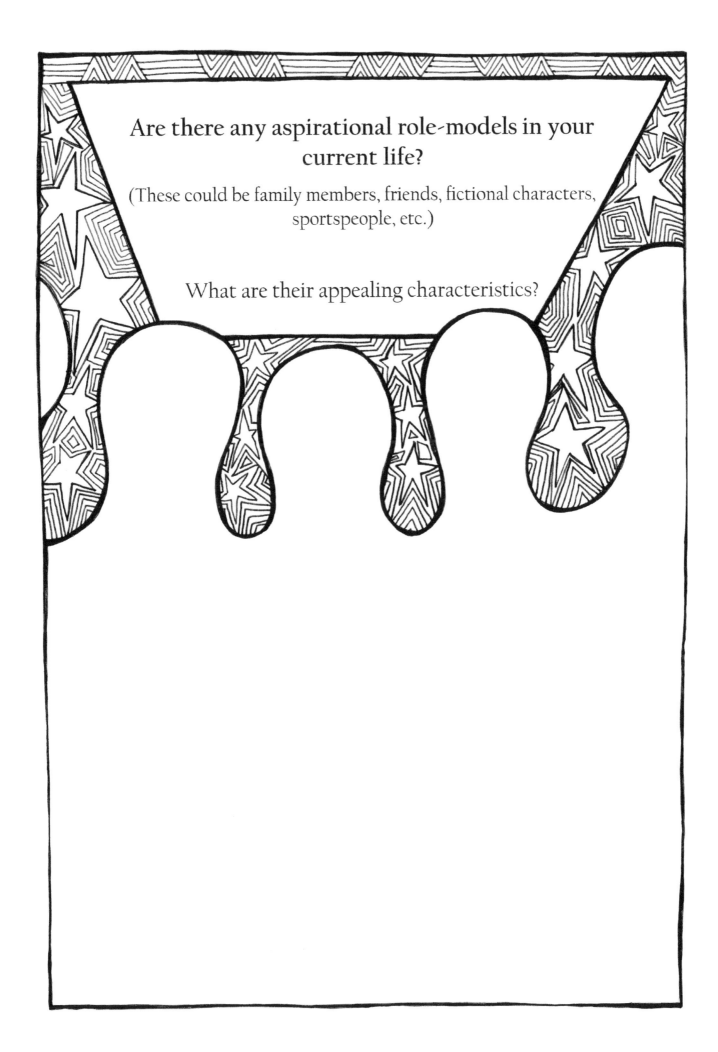

Are there any aspirational role-models in your current life?

(These could be family members, friends, fictional characters, sportspeople, etc.)

What are their appealing characteristics?

If you were to draw or describe **_stress_**, what would this look like?

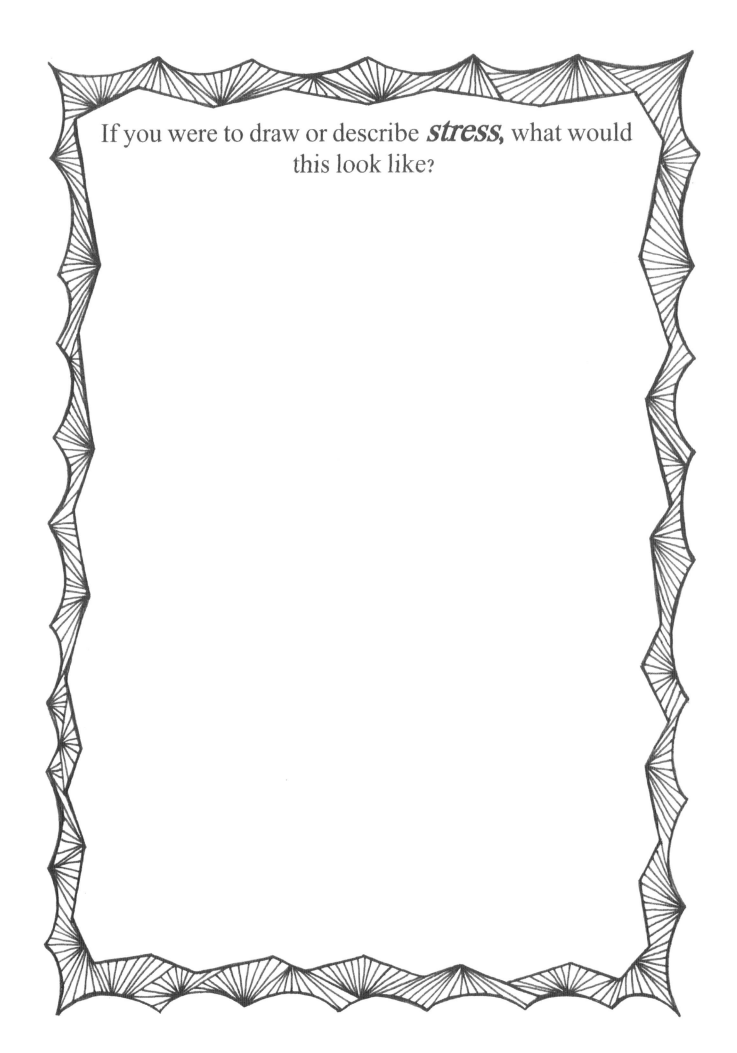

If *stress* became absent from **your life,** how would you notice?

How would **others** notice?

Contentment:

What would this look like in your life?

Contentment:

Is this important to you?

What would the opposite look like?

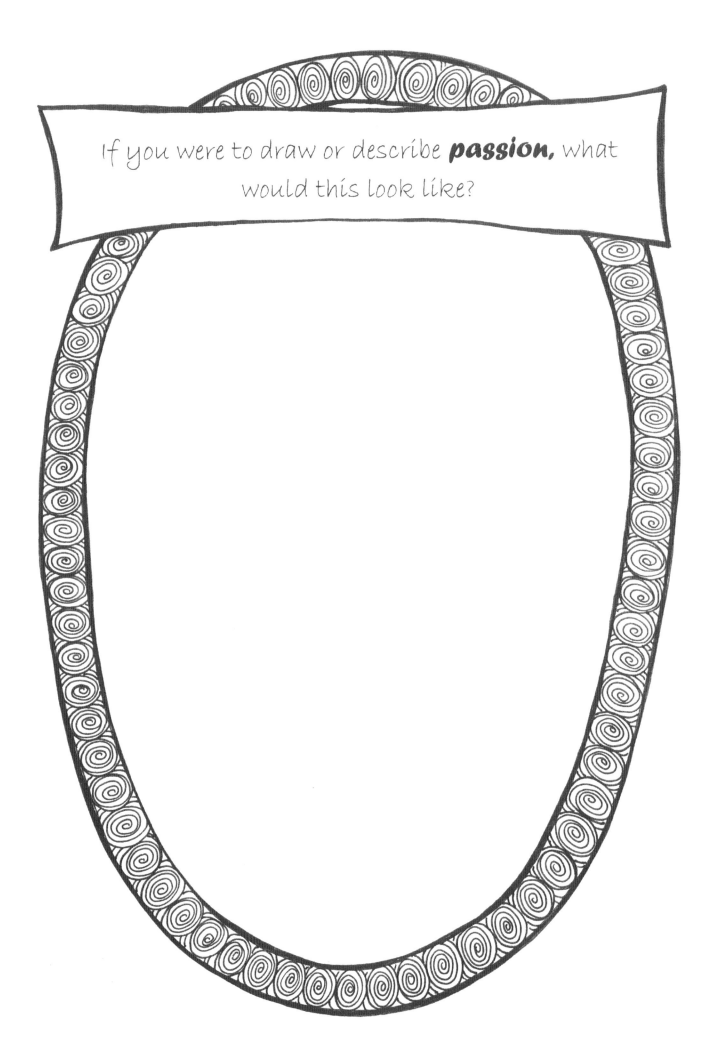

If you were to draw or describe **passion,** what would this look like?

If you were to describe or draw *loss*, what would this look like?

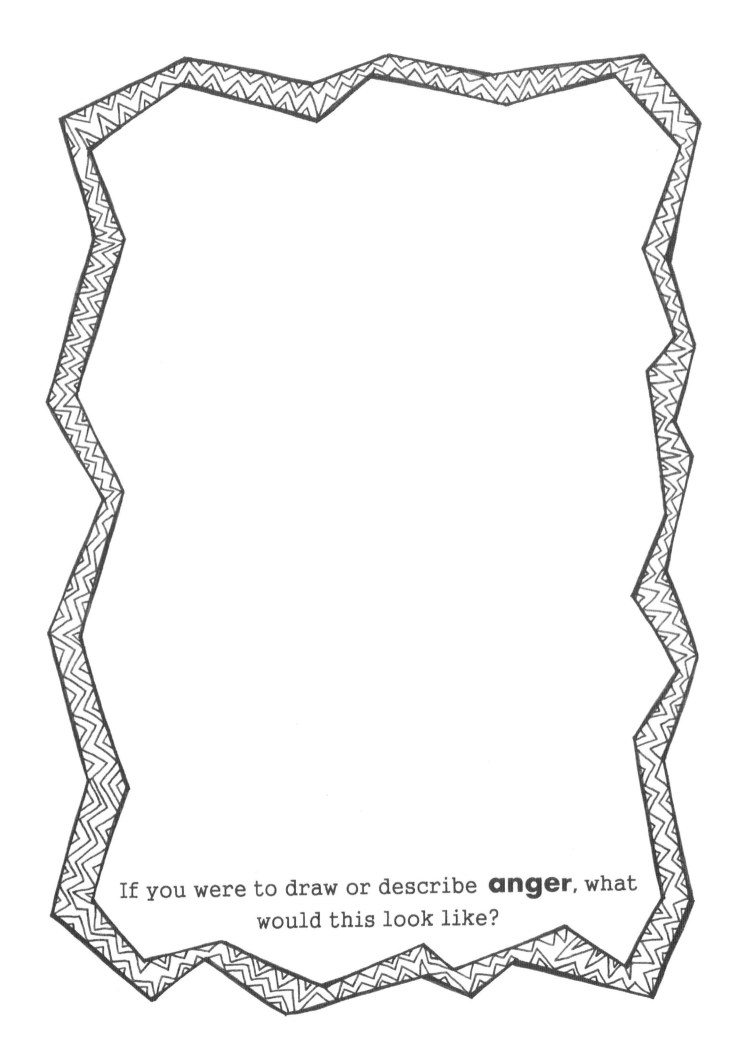

If you were to draw or describe **anger**, what would this look like?

If you were to draw or describe **fear,** what would this look like?

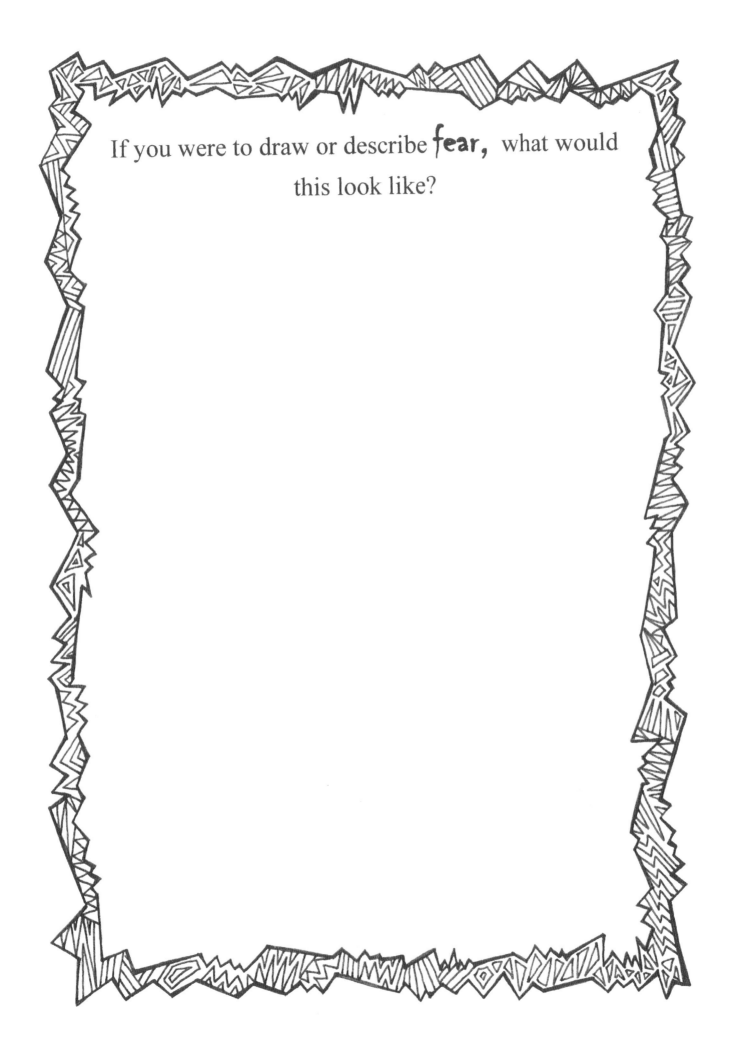

Divide the circle into segments to show the levels in your life of…

joy　　　adventure　　　contentment　　　adversity

excitement　　　adventure　　　relaxation

Ways I can **be kind** to myself today...

What does the **light at the end** of the tunnel look like?

Draw or describe how you'd like to be,

1 year from now...

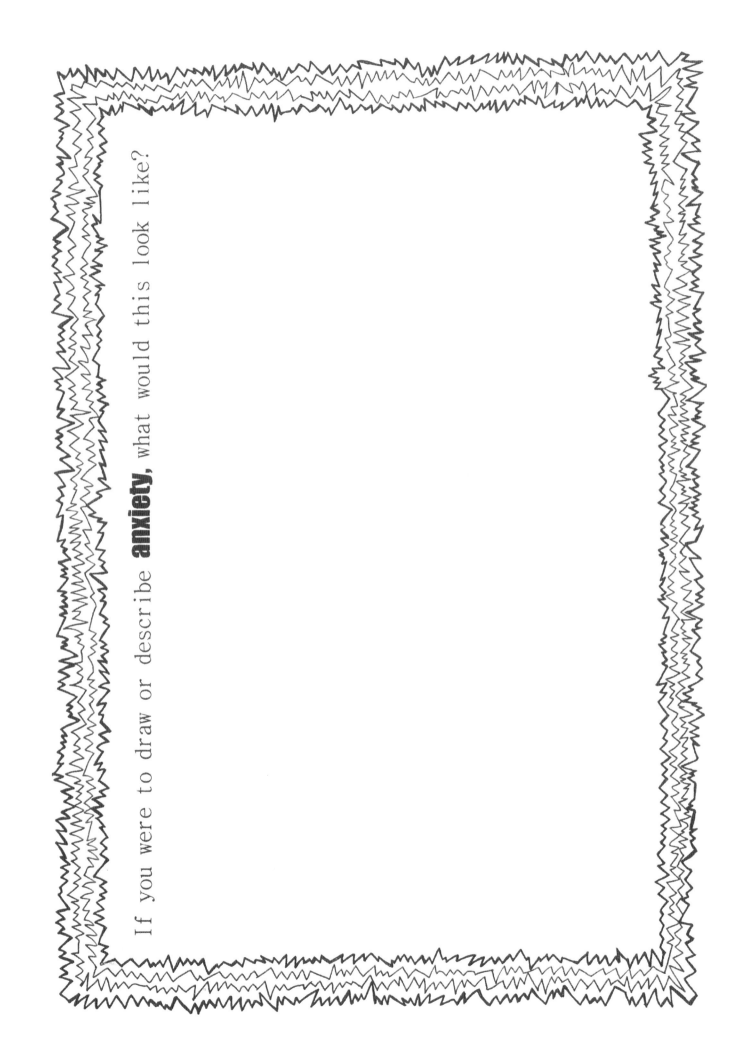

If you were to draw or describe **anxiety,** what would this look like?

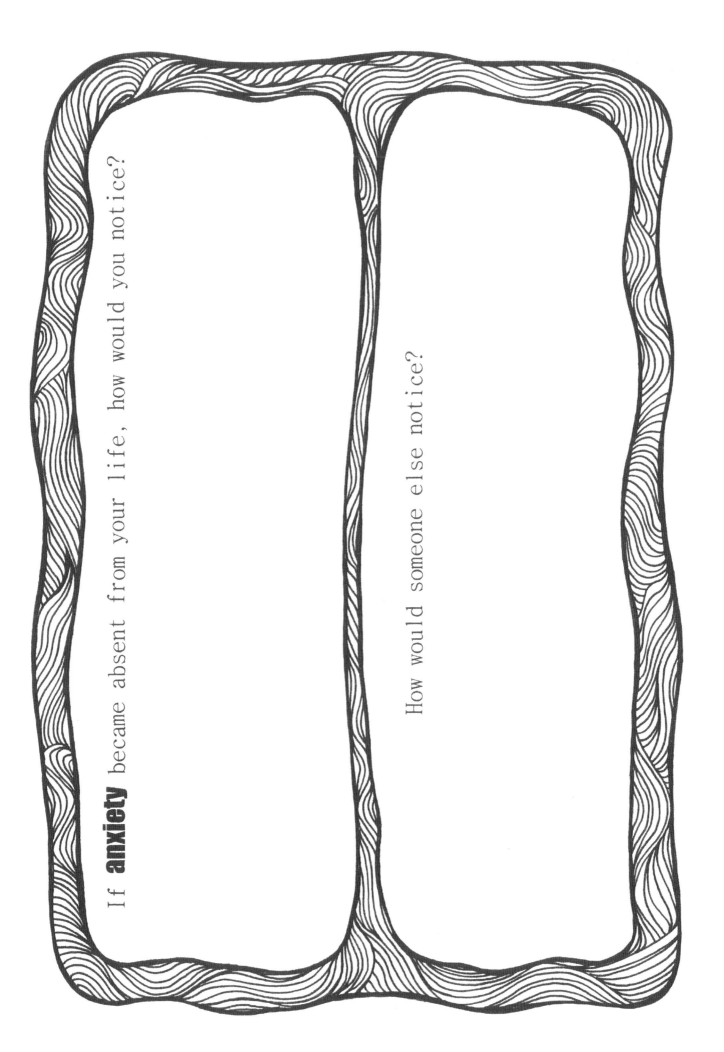

If **anxiety** became absent from your life, how would you notice?

How would someone else notice?

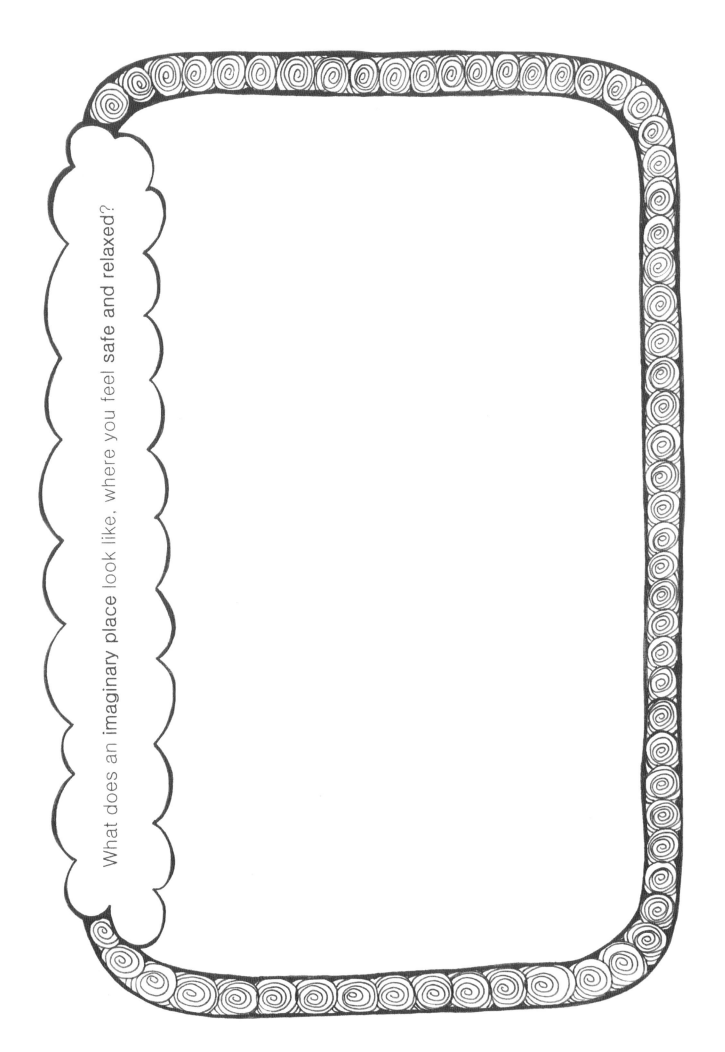

What does an imaginary place look like, where you feel safe and relaxed?

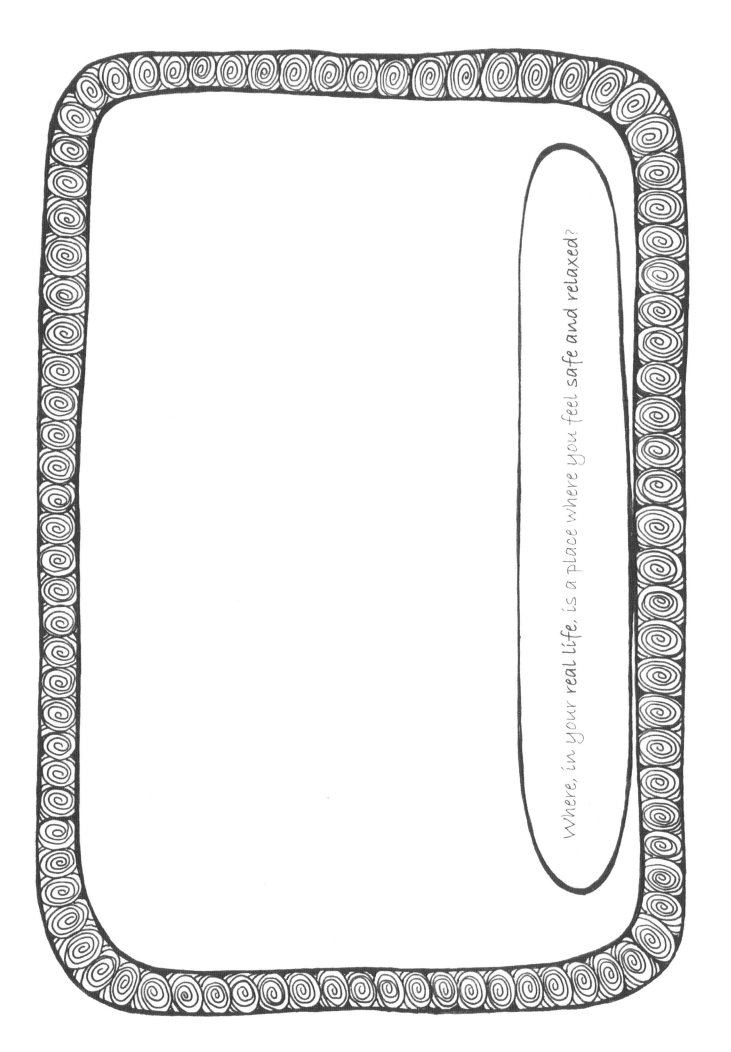

Where, in your real life, is a place where you feel safe and relaxed?

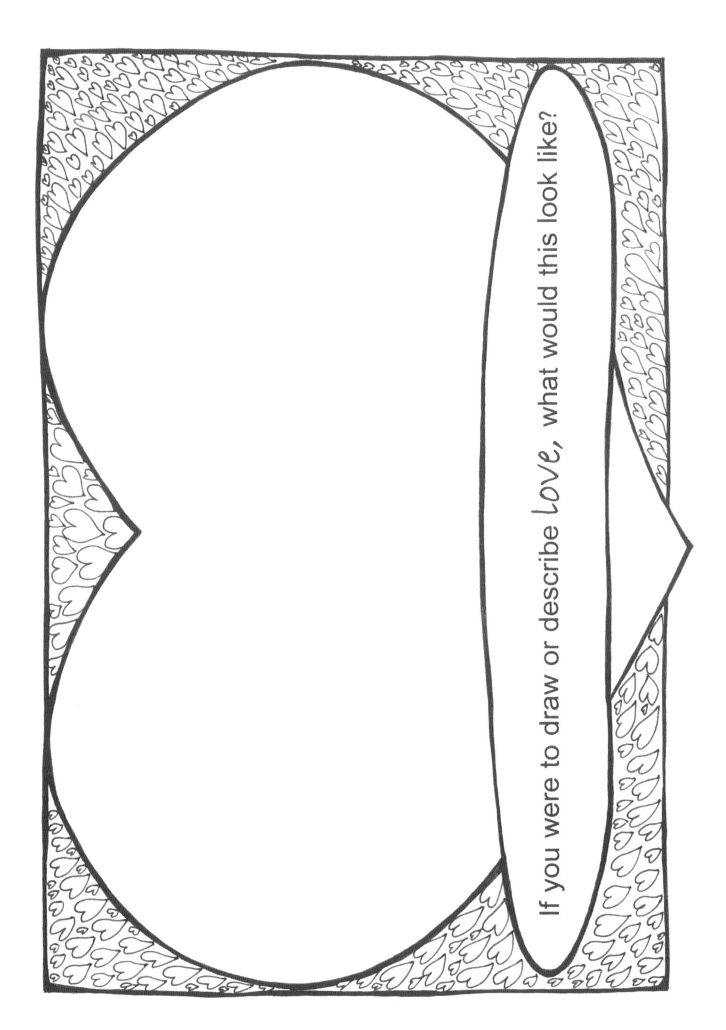

If you were to draw or describe *Love*, what would this look like?

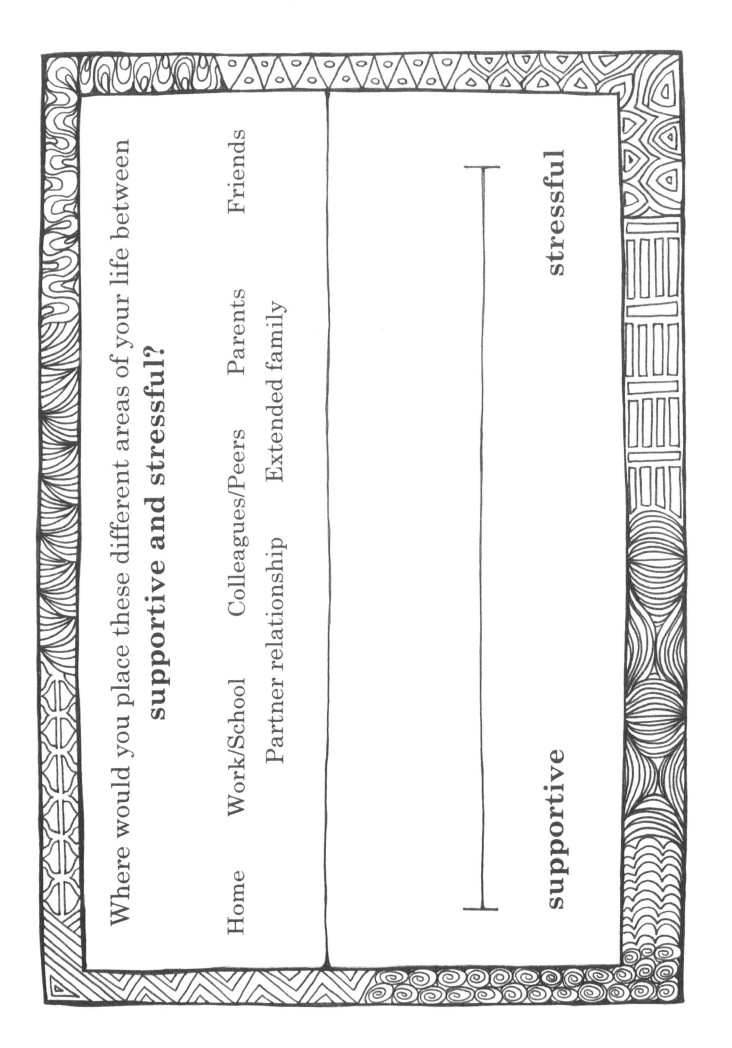

Where would you place these different areas of your life between **supportive and stressful?**

Home   Work/School   Colleagues/Peers   Parents   Friends

Partner relationship   Extended family

stressful

supportive

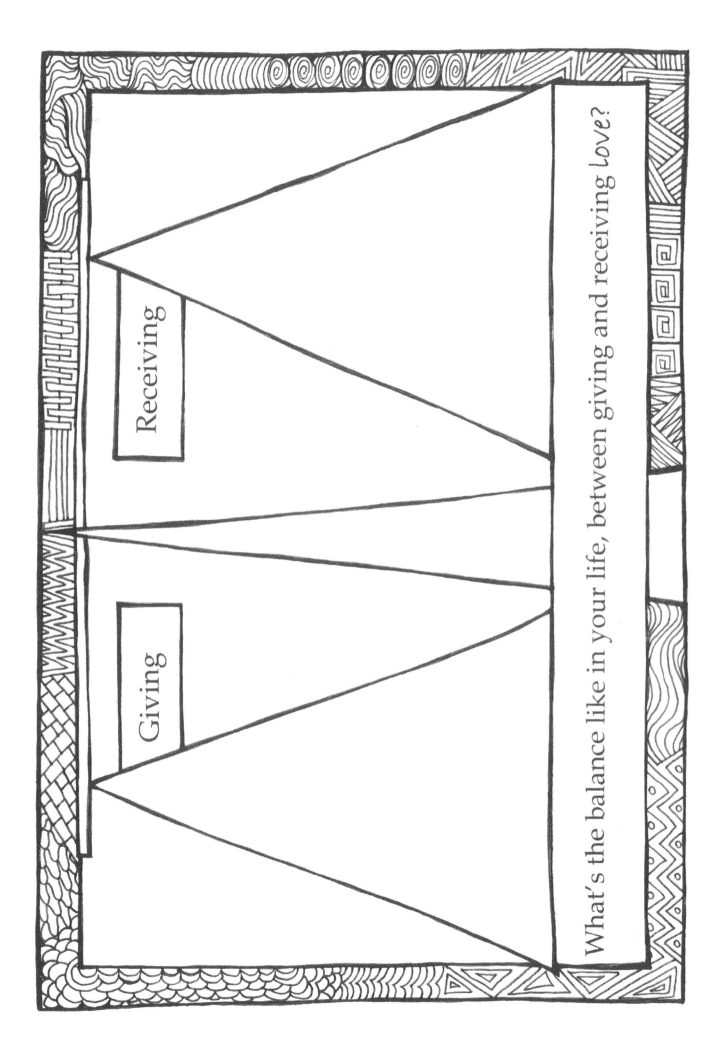

Receiving

Giving

What's the balance like in your life, between giving and receiving *love*?

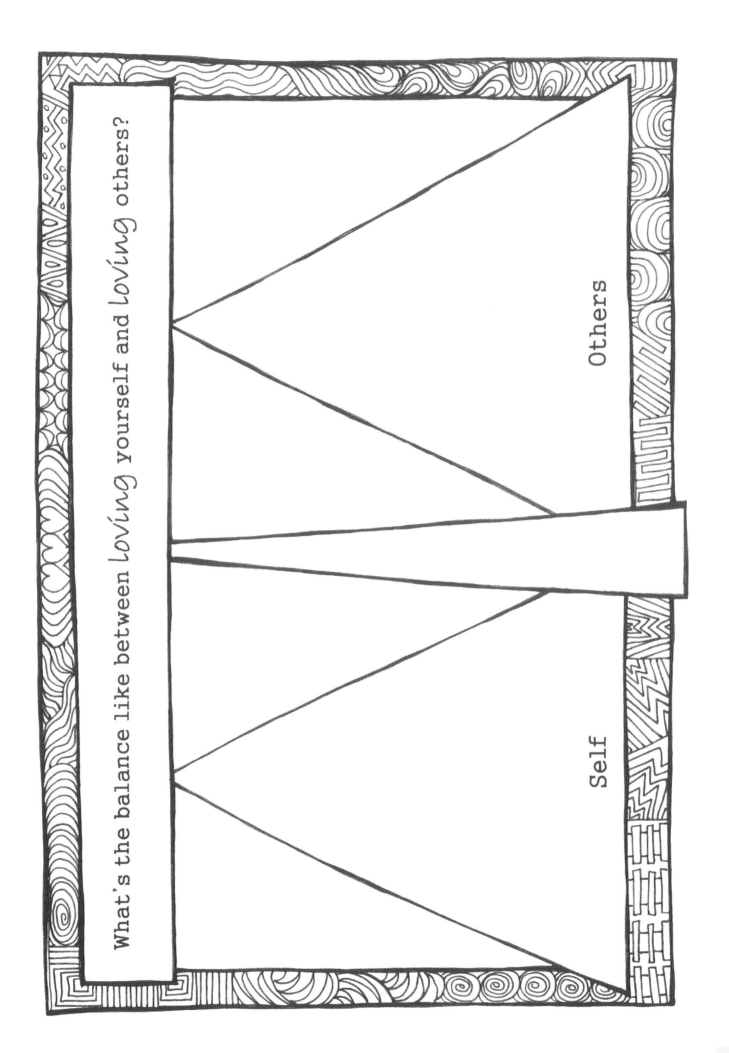

What's the balance like between *loving* yourself and *loving* others?

Others

Self

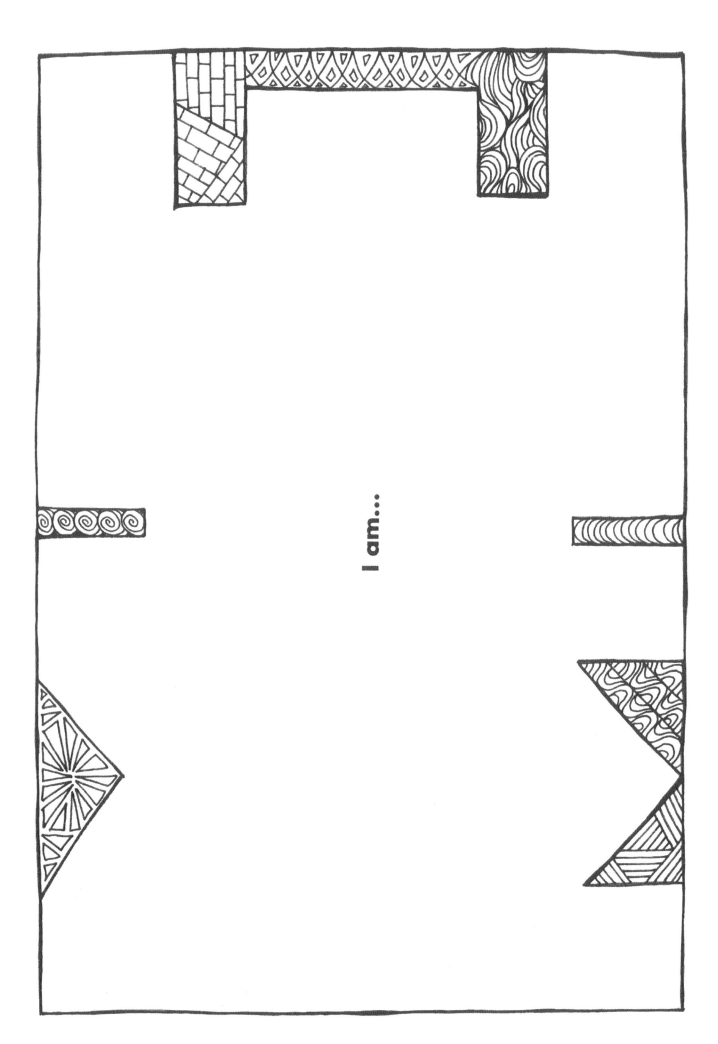

I am...

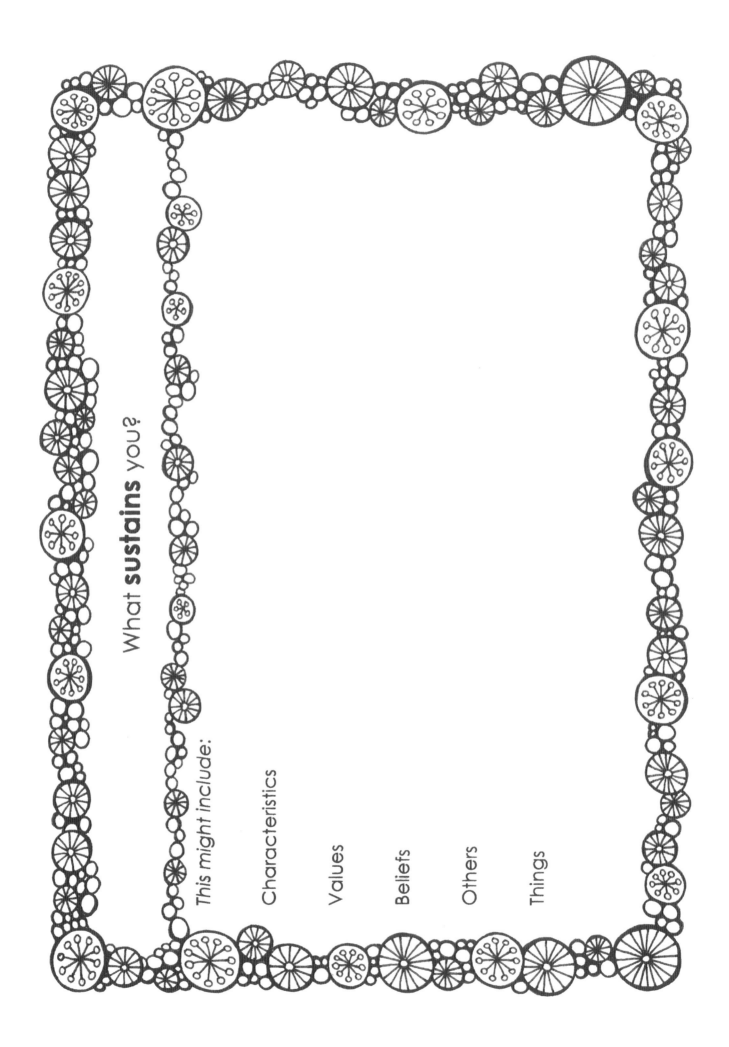

What **sustains** you?

This might include:

Characteristics

Values

Beliefs

Others

Things

Chapter 3

Reflecting

When experiencing high levels of stress, unconscious processes can dominate, whereby people revert back to unhelpful patterns of thinking, feeling and behaviours. Exploration into memories and experiences can help provide insights into unconscious processes and the level to which they may influence our current lives.

Although our sense of self evolves as we grow older, there are some fundamental parts that, in psychodynamic terms, we internalise in childhood. This is explained by Thomas (1996, p.294):

> A large component of internal worlds are introjected versions of other people and relationships, known as internal object relations. As objects and object relations are introjected they carry with them pre-verbal social 'messages' about values, gender and power relations. It is largely from these internal figures and relationships, and our identifications with them, that selfhood is constructed.

Many of the worksheets in this chapter focus on exploration into early experiences and memories, in order to identify some of these internalised messages, which may or may not be helpful to us in adulthood.

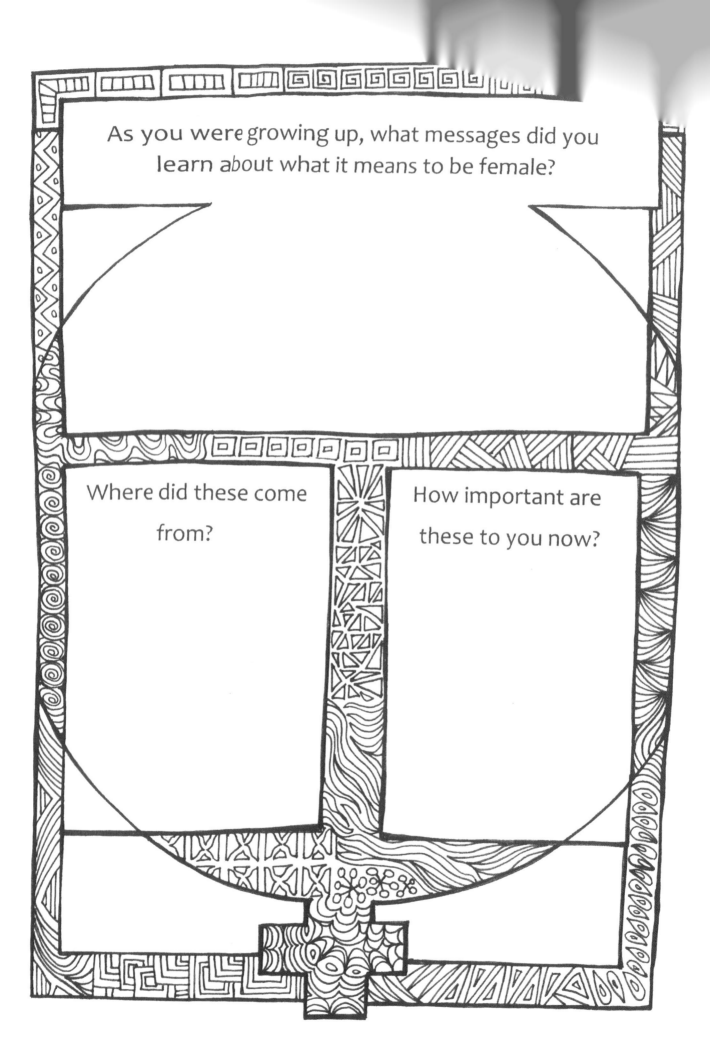

As you were growing up, what messages did you learn about what it means to be female?

Where did these come from?

How important are these to you now?

One of my **saddest memories** is...

As you were growing up, what messages did you learn about what it means to be male?

Where did these come from?

How important are these to you now?

(1)

What was your **favourite toy** from childhood?

(2)

Why was this special?

Who gave this to you?

What emotional memories do you

associate with it?

What were your favourite **childhood games**?

Did you prefer **solitary or team** games, or a mixture of both?

Do you enjoy **playing games** now?

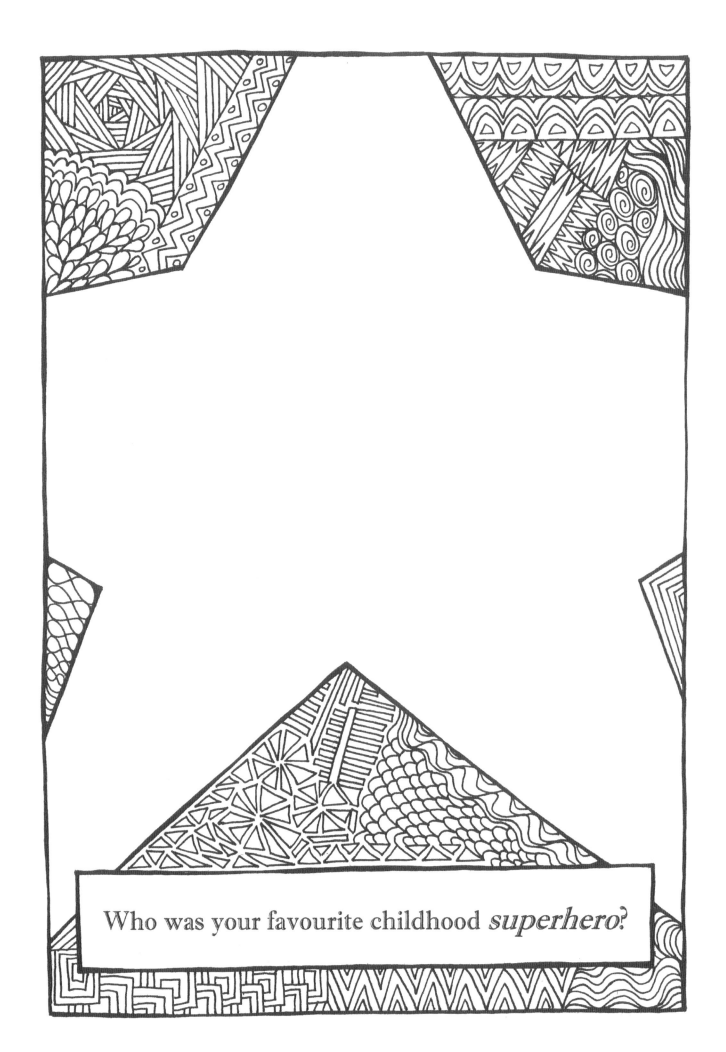

Who was your favourite childhood *superhero*?

(1)

What were your **hopes and dreams** for your adult life, when you were younger?

(2) Have any been actualised already?

How do these compare with your

hopes and dreams now?

Draw or describe *yourself*

5 years ago...

One of my *happiest memories* from adulthood is...

One of my **happiest memories** from childhood is...

A difficult memory from childhood is...

A difficult memory from

adulthood is...

How influential or important are these to you now?

Where did these come from?

As you grew up, what were the messages you learnt about yourself?

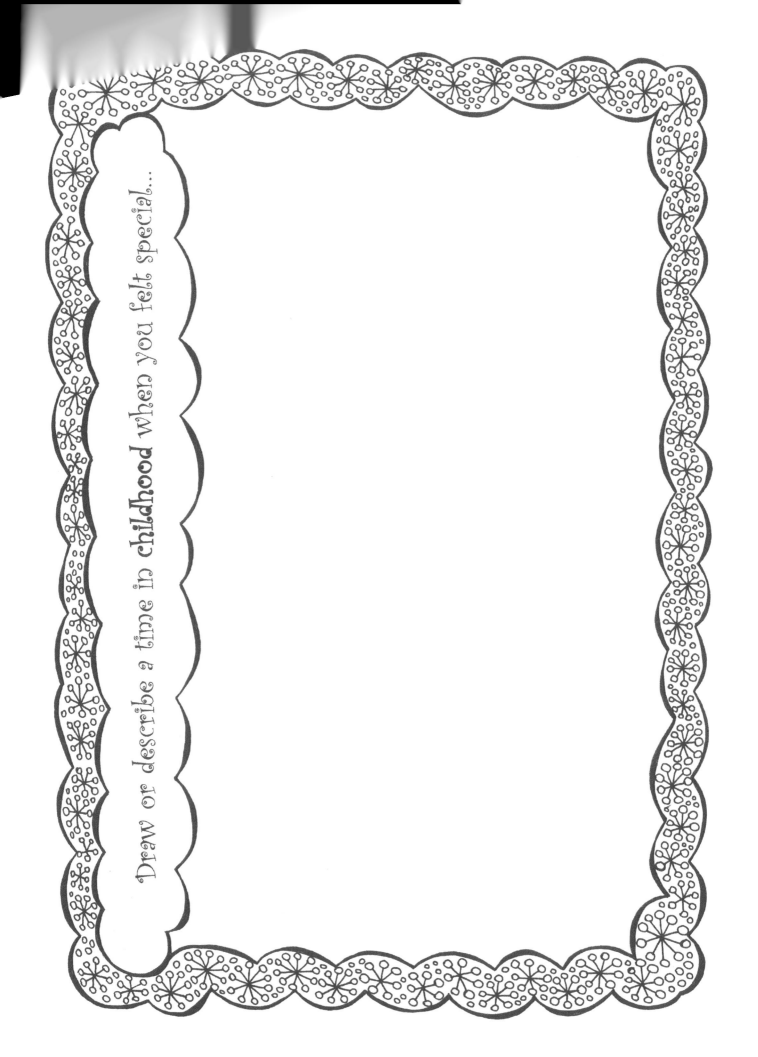

Draw or describe a time in childhood when you felt special....

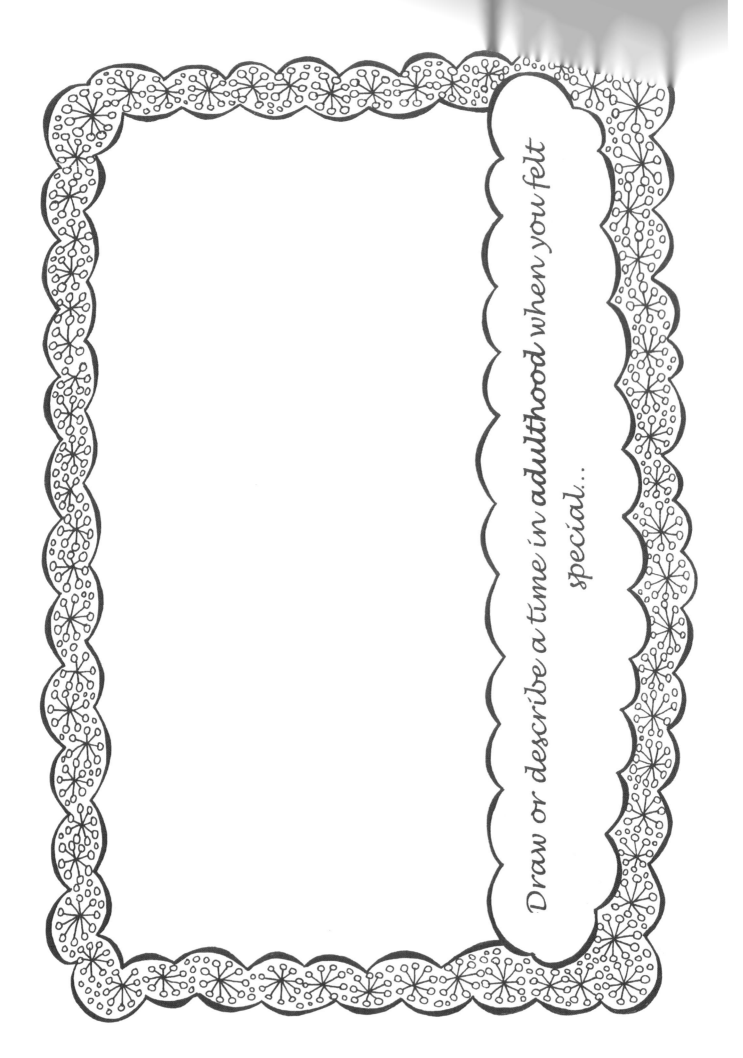

Draw or describe a time in adulthood when you felt special...

A **life-changing moment** in my adulthood was....

A life-changing moment in my childhood was...

Chapter 4

Journaling

Recording thoughts and feelings is a technique often used in CBT to help identify problematic aspects, elicit changes and to clarify goals. Writing in *Therapy Today*, Jonathan Hales (2014, pp.28–29) states how counselling is likely to have a more productive outcome if 'we work with what's going on in our clients' daily lives and help them to realise their own strengths and resources'. Keeping a journal is an effective way of recognising and communicating such aspects of daily life.

In their book *CBT Worksheets*, Drs James Manning and Nicola Ridgeway describe some of the benefits of diary keeping: 'As with all diaries, thoughts, feeling and behaviour based records encourage clients to increase distance from their problems and to look at things from a more balanced perspective' (2016, p.6).

Art therapist Cathy A. Malchiodi believes journaling with images is an effective way of coping with challenging times and difficult emotions. She herself has kept a journal for many years and states how 'visual journals enable me to let feelings go and to get through difficult transitions in my life' (2007, p.153).

The worksheets in this chapter invite people to focus on the content of their daily lives, some about behaviour, some about thoughts and feelings. Practitioners may choose to make up a collection of pages to constitute a journal using the most appropriate worksheets for an individual client.

MY DIARY

Week beginning:

Goals for this week:

Draw or describe how you're feeling in this moment...

CERTIFICATE

of

today's achievements:

Today, I'm going to appreciate...

If you were to draw or describe your **day,** this would look like...

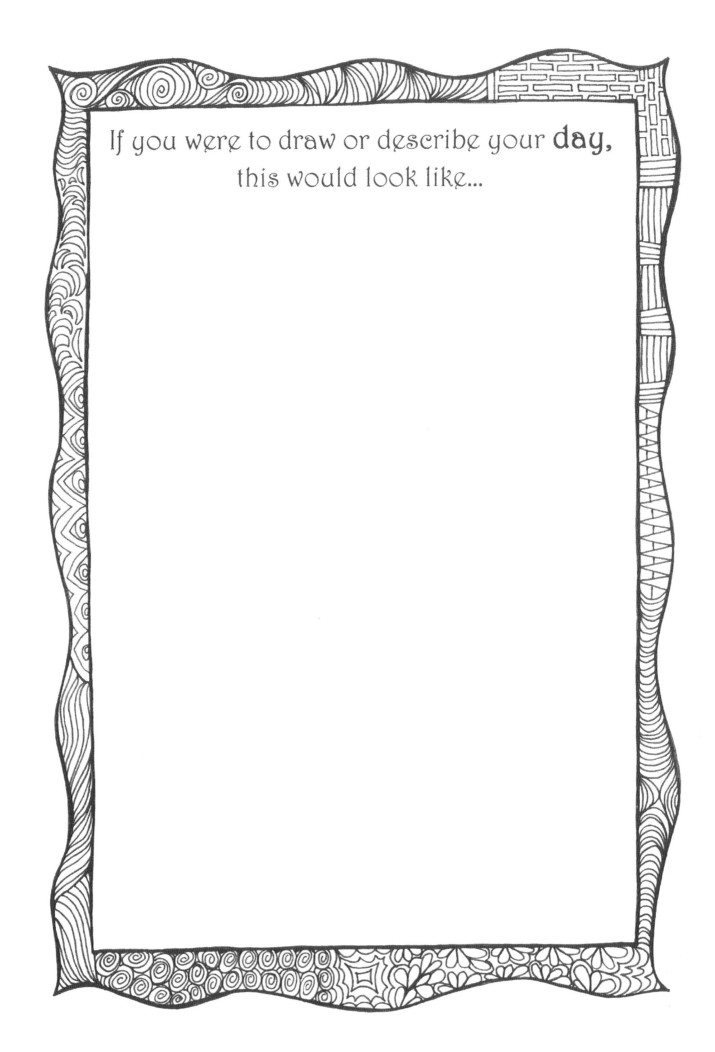

Positive moments *from my day:*

Tomorrow

is going to look like...

If I had no **responsibilities or commitments** for the whole day tomorrow, I would like to spend my time...

(1)

Divide the circle into segments, to show how your time is currently spent:

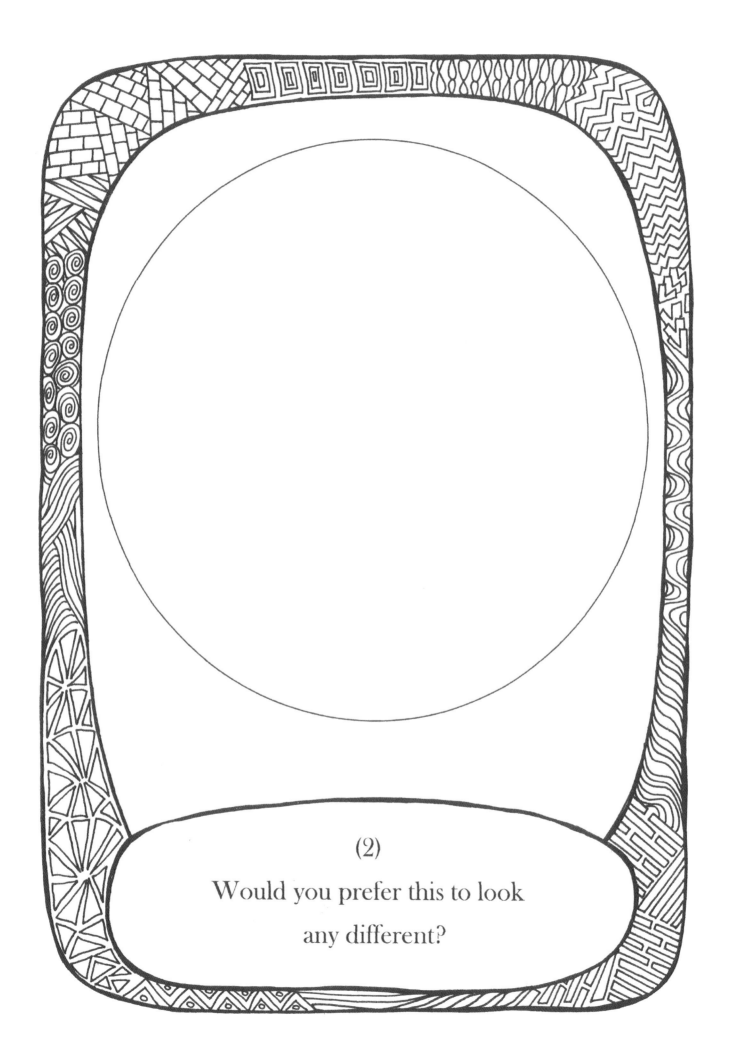

(2)

Would you prefer this to look

any different?

Chapter 5

Metaphor

In the search to get to know ourselves better, it can often help to use metaphors to gain a fresh perspective. Describing and comparing our character or life with something completely different can bring about new information and insights. In their book *Symbol, Story and Ceremony: Using Metaphor in Individual and Family Therapy*, Combs and Freedman state:

> A metaphor is something that stands for something else... A metaphor always communicates on at least two levels...each one adding richness of meaning. It is this multiplicity of dimensions that distinguishes metaphors from 'straight' communication. We use the word 'symbol' to refer to the smallest units of metaphor – words, objects, mental images, and the like – in which a richness of meaning is crystallised. (1990, p.xiv)

They also describe how psychoanalyst Erik Erikson was a pioneer in his use of symbols and stories to 'pursue therapeutic goals indirectly. The creative use of indirection is essential in allowing for newness and evolution in psychotherapy' (1990, p.xvii). In *Understanding the Self* Richard Stevens writes:

> The use of metaphor is one of the most important means we have of extending our understanding. What a metaphor does is to place a concept in the context of another concept and, by so doing, alter its meaning and implications. In this way, the juxtaposition or fusion of the two concepts involved often creates an emergent third meaning which is more than just the sum of the other two. (Stevens 1996, p.170)

The worksheets in this chapter aim to facilitate and generate new ideas and develop different perspectives about ourselves and our lives. They can act as conversation starters, inspiring further curiosity from a practitioner with regards to aspects such as other qualities about a chosen image, symbol or piece of writing. Examples could be about texture, size, shape, scent, robustness and so on.

If I were a river, it would look like...

If you were to draw or describe yourself as a mode of transport, what would this look like?

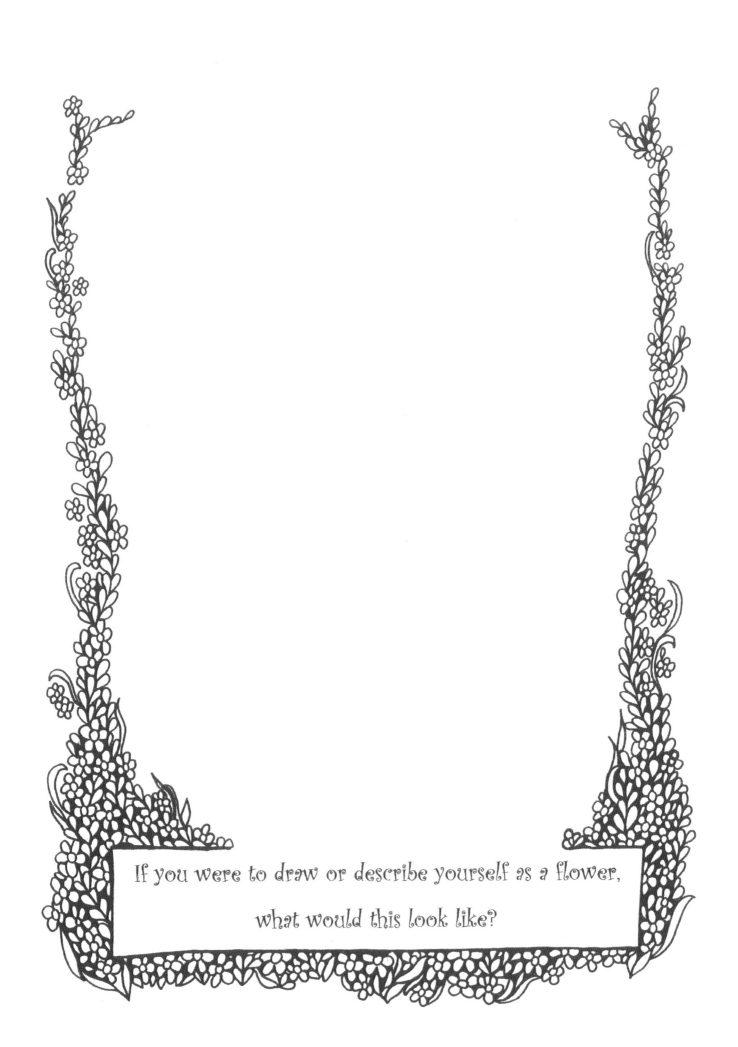

If you were to draw or describe yourself as a flower, what would this look like?

If I were the weather today...

If I were an animal, I would look like...

If you were a **musical instrument**, what would this look like?

If I were something edible, I would be...

If this point in your life were **a door/gateway**,
what would this look like?

If I were in or on **an ocean,**
what would this look like?

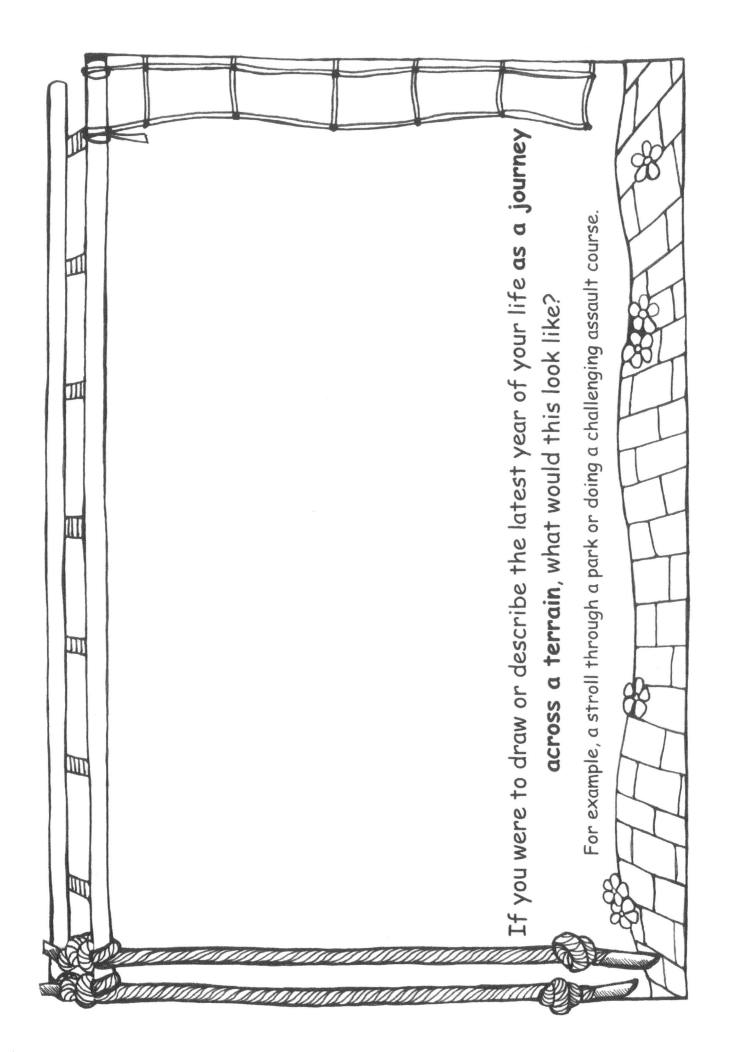

If you were to draw or describe the latest year of your life as a journey across a terrain, what would this look like?

For example, a stroll through a park or doing a challenging assault course.

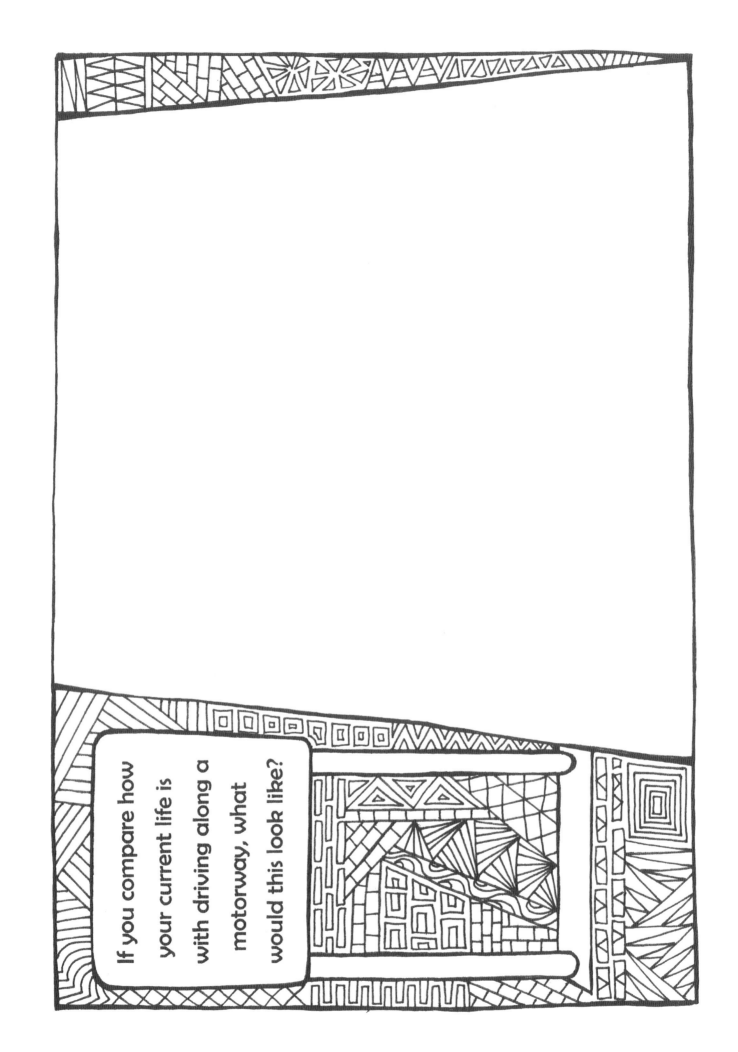

If you compare how your current life is with driving along a motorway, what would this look like?

If you were a part of a forest, what would this look like?

References

Bandura, A. (1982) 'Self-efficacy mechanism in human agency.' *American Psychologist* 37: 122–147.

Baumeister, R.F. (1991) *Meanings in Life*. New York, NY: Guilford Press.

Beck, A.T. (1967) *Depression: Causes and Treatment*. Philadelphia, PA: University of Pennsylvania Press.

Beck, A.T., Epstein, N. and Harrison, R. (1983) 'Cognition, attitudes and personality dimensions in depression.' *British Journal of Psychotherapy* 1: 1–16.

Bolton, G. (2000) *The Therapeutic Potential of Creative Writing: Writing Myself*. London: Jessica Kingsley Publishers.

Burton, M. and Davey, T. (2003) 'The psychodynamic paradigm.' In R. Woolfe, W. Dryden and S. Strawbridge (eds) *Handbook of Counselling Psychology*. London: Sage.

Charura, D. and Paul, S. (eds) (2014) *The Therapeutic Relationship Handbook*. Milton Keynes: Open University Press.

Combs, G. and Freedman, J. (1990) *Symbol, Story and Ceremony: Using Metaphor in Individual and Family Therapy*. London: Norton.

Edwards, B. (2008) *The New Drawing on the Right Side of the Brain*. London: HarperCollins.

Fisher, P. (2014) 'The opportunities, challenges, and complexities of maintaining a therapeutic relationship within the creative therapies.' In D. Charura and S. Paul (eds) *The Therapeutic Relationship Handbook*. Milton Keynes: Open University Press.

Goleman, D. (1996) *Emotional Intelligence: Why it Can Matter More Than IQ*. London: Bloomsbury.

Hales, J. (2014) 'Working with our clients' worlds.' *Therapy Today* 25(10): 28–29.

Malchiodi, C.A. (2007) *The Art Therapy Sourcebook*. London: McGraw Hill.

Manning, J. and Ridgeway, N. (2016) *CBT Worksheets*. Milton Keynes: CreateSpace Independent Publishing Platform.

Scott, M.J. and Dryden, W. (2003) 'The cognitive behavioural paradigm.' In R. Woolfe, W. Dryden and S. Strawbridge (eds) *Handbook of Counselling Psychology*. London: Sage.

Simon, G. (2011) *Writing (As) Systemic Practice*. Professional Doctorate in Systemic Practice, University of Bedfordshire.

Stevens, R. (ed.) (1996) *Understanding the Self*. London: Sage.

Stevens, R. and Wetherall, M. (1996) 'The self in the modern world: Drawing together the threads.' In R. Stevens (ed.) *Understanding the Self*. London: Sage.

Strawbridge, S. and Woolfe, R. (2003) 'Counselling psychology in context.' In R. Woolfe, W. Dryden and S. Strawbridge (eds) *Handbook of Counselling Psychology*. London: Sage.

Thomas, K. (1996) 'The defensive self: A psychodynamic perspective.' In R. Stevens (ed.) *Understanding the Self*. London: Sage.

Trower, P., Casey, A. and Dryden, W. (1988) *Cognitive Behavioural Counselling in Action*. London: Sage.

THE ART
ACTIVITY BOOK FOR
PSYCHOTHERAPEUTIC
WORK

The accompanying PDF can be downloaded from
https://library.jkp.com/redeem using the code GUESTPSYCH

by the same author

The CBT Art Activity Book
100 illustrated handouts for creative therapeutic work
Jennifer Guest
ISBN 978 1 84905 665 6
eISBN 978 1 78450 168 6

The Art Activity Book for Relational Work
100 illustrated therapeutic worksheets to use with individuals, couples and families
Jennifer Guest
ISBN 978 1 78592 160 5
eISBN 978 1 78450 428 1

of related interest

Raising Self-Esteem in Adults
An Eclectic Approach with Art Therapy, CBT and DBT Based Techniques
Susan I. Buchalter
ISBN 978 1 84905 966 4
eISBN 978 0 85700 821 3